"Focusing on radical empathy, love and justice, Peter Bridge offers an accessible and compelling paradigm for honest self-reflection. Interweaving his experiences of the rich cultures, as well as the tragic divisions of his native South Africa, with added texture from his years of ministry in the US, he invites us to work against our ingrained biases, our deference to entrenched power structures, and our unresolved traumas in order to embrace the fullness of our shared humanity. "

Celene Ibrahim, Ph.D.
Religious Studies Scholar; Author of *Islam and Monotheism, Women and Gender in the Qur'an,* and *One Nation, Indivisible*

Faculty Member in Religious Studies and Philosophy and Muslim Chaplain at Groton School.

"Justice-Love is a book to be experienced — not just read. It is a gem for anyone serious about transforming their compassion into loving action for a more just world."

The Rev. Tracie L. Bartholomew
Bishop, NJ Synod, ELCA

"When we love and do justice we will live in peace. We will live in the spirit of 'ubuntu,' which is our shared humanity. Bridge's Justice-Love *shows us the way. ... Come back to it often."*

The Right Rev. Charles May
Bishop, Diocese of Highveld, South Africa

"Peter's self-reflective approach allows readers of any faith to look into the mirror and ensure we are truly operating with loving regard for others when pursuing the work of repairing the world."

Rabbi Andrew K. Mandel, Founder
Tzedek Box: Supporting the Timeless Jewish Call for Justice

JUSTICE-LOVE

Discover It in Stillness
Grow It in Shared Humanity
Activate It to Heal Your Community

To dear Natalie,

Peter J. Bridge

Peter J. Bridge

Partners in justice-seeking !

With love,

Peter

United Writers Press
Asheville, N.C.

United Writers Press
Asheville, N.C.
www.UWPnew.com

ISBN: 978-1-961813-48-9 (trade paperback)

Scripture Quotations: are from the *New Revised Standard Version of the Bible* (NRSV), the Jewish Publication Society's *Tanakh, The Holy Scriptures: The New JPS Translation according to the Traditional* Hebrew Text. (JPS Tanakh 1985), and *The Qur'an, A New Translation* by M.A.S. Abdel Haleem, Oxford World's Classics, Oxford University Press 2016.

Cover art and design by United Writers Press.

Printed in the USA.

To Jane

Contents

Foreword

I have known Peter Bridge for 10 years and have personally benefited from his guidance and caring. Living in Camden, NJ and, having spent much of my work life in Trenton, it means a lot to me that he truly cares about those two cities, their residents and especially their youth. *And* that he cares about justice in all settings—whether urban or not.

Justice-Love is an excellent book for self-reflection and for discovering and facing our hidden intentions. Being open to those different from ourselves is the key to truly connecting with them. And that openness requires that we look deeply and caringly into their situation and history. With examples from his life in South Africa—and his career in the US—Peter invites us to probe our own thoughts and emotions if we want to connect with groups and individuals in a just and loving way. I could especially relate to the suggestion that we liberate ourselves from being "stuck" in our own culture. Transparency and openness to other cultures require a willingness to let go of the "known" and venture into the "unknown." Our future-oriented ambition often blocks Justice-Love. It takes us away from being in the present moment—which is the moment of true presence and connection with another human being.

That really spoke to me. When I'm too focused on what comes next, I rob myself of the gift of being truly present. So I rob myself also of a chance to connect with another person. Human beings want love, dignity and justice. This timely book shows how true presence and humbly learning about each other lead us to Justice-Love.

Peter describes our "Shared Humanity" as "Love's Original Family." He truly lives in that family. Keep this book as your companion as you strive to activate Justice-Love in yourself and your community.

Elyse Smith
Street Leader Director
Urban Promise, Trenton, NJ
2011-2023

Preface

I've heard an awful lot of sermons and read a great many books encouraging me to be a more loving person. When I read the next book or listen to the next sermon, I sometimes feel disappointed in myself because I have not made much progress at all. Somehow, it's just not that easy to put it into practice.

The same can be said of justice. I want to be a justice-seeker, a person who works to eliminate injustice and to make the world a more just place. I agree enthusiastically with books and lectures about this and am often greatly energized. But the energy is often short-lived. My resolutions disappear until the next convincing book or talk.

There's a missing ingredient, I think—a fire for love *and* justice that is not so easily extinguished—a heart-conviction. A heart conviction gets its energy, durability and action from something that happens inside a person. It does not depend on something external like a book or a fine sermon. A "mere" head-conviction may be strengthened by an accumulation of facts, figures and strong words. But those additional layers often distract from the internal fanning of the flames that energizes loving action. My conviction about the need for the internal fanning of the flames is what has inspired me to write this book.

Knowledge accumulation does not enflame hearts. Getting the "heart-fire" started needs what all fires need—a quiet invisible "oxygen" assisted by a gentle breeze. The "oxygen" for the enkindling of our hearts is the internal work we do in the stillness of our hearts. It's our willingness to be self-reflective so that we can have the courage to discover our truth, who we really are "warts and all." The fire in our hearts also needs the gentle breeze, and sometimes the not-so-gentle buffeting wind of accountability.

Enkindling our hearts all by ourselves is pretty much of a non-starter. We need to be held accountable for our attitudes and actions. Feedback from our lover, our neighbor, our friend, is essential for the testing of our heart-convictions. Without community feedback, there is danger that the flames we fan are flames of arrogance, self-importance and a self-righteous refusal to listen and learn.

As a relationship therapist, I often needed to remind people about the difference between "declaring" love for someone and actually "acting" lovingly. Partners began to make progress only when the love we focused on was not a noun but a verb, not a mere feeling but an action aimed at respect and fairness. We began to define love as the caring way a person ACTS toward another when they feel joy at another's joy or compassion at another's hurt.

Similar nudging towards an active definition of love was needed in my conflict resolution work with groups. There was little progress until one group found a way to genuinely care deeply about the underlying feelings and hurts of the other group. And then consider what ACTIONS might help.

In the early years of the anti-apartheid struggle in South Africa, an esteemed colleague and theologian Albert Nolan urged us never to forget the crucial connection between love and justice (Nolan, 1986). He suggested the term **"Justice-Love"** might help keep us focused on this robust and division-healing kind of love. Hence the title of this book. Justice-Love is a love which proceeds out of the very deepest kind of human compassion, a radical empathy that is focused on the feelings and needs of another human being instead of what we think they deserve. It's an empathy that puts effort into trying to understand the reasons for those feelings and needs, and then takes loving action aimed at healing and remediation. It requires self-honesty and self-reflection-and a willingness to be non-defensive and non-judgmental.

Though not prominent in my religious upbringing, radical empathy is an important part of my Judeo-Christian heritage. Hebrew prophets insist on periodic debt forgiveness, radical, no questions asked. Jesus' mind-blowing parables have a father welcoming home his irresponsible, prodigal son with a feast instead of punishment, and also workers arriving late in the day being paid the same as others who started on time. This kind of empathy, that nudges us toward Justice-Love, is easily lost in a tangle of lesser concerns. This book keeps radical empathy front and center.

Justice-Love does not grow out of pity, occasional warm feelings, pseudo-agreement, or the kind of "charity" that arises out of guilt. Frankly, neither does it follow easily on the exhortations of an enthusiastic preacher, nor the righteous anger of a sincere activist. These may stimulate good intentions and the urge to be a loving person but the formidable inner work remains to be done!

Our fellow human beings are our brothers and sisters in humanity. They should never be mere objects of our pity and "charity." Genuine healing love starts with self-knowledge and humility. It is nurtured and strengthened by a deep gratitude for our very existence. That kind of gratitude makes one want to share life's blessings with everybody else — no exceptions. To sustain that love and have it flow into loving action, the lover needs to work hard to know and understand the person or group she wants to love.

Yes, the hard work of love is very different from an eloquent exhortation to love. It's different also from our own inner aspirations or good intentions. I am tremendously inspired by Martin Luther King's vision of the "Beloved Community." But I do worry sometimes that we'll always just be talking about it and dreaming about it if we don't find a way, each one of us, to get down to the nitty-gritty hard work that can actualize love in a person or a community.

This isn't a long book. For years, I have complained about long, dense books. I'm not sure who first said it but I love the saying: "Inside every fat book is a thin book desperately trying to get out!" Hopefully, this is the thin book that has been trying to emerge through me during a long career which has spanned a broad range of ministry and therapy settings.

The birth pangs of this book parallel the birth pangs of my many "born again" experiences. I have happily been "born again" rather often—out of a rather "traditional" priestly role into a more "prophetic" and "political" kind of priesthood, out of Roman Catholicism into the Episcopal Church USA, out of celibacy into marriage, from teaching to preaching, from community-organizing social work to clinical social work. And the birth pangs continue!

But the core of my career was an over 30-year spell as a pastor and clinical social worker doing therapy and consulting in both secular and interfaith settings. It was during those years in personal sessions and group lectures and seminars, on both sides of the podium, that I was profoundly touched and educated by my "healer" colleagues who put their trust in me as their therapeutic companion, mentor and guide. Out of that grew a conviction that there are only a handful of key growth resources for persons who want to be justice-makers.

Who is this book for? Anyone who has struggled to keep their resolutions about being more lovingly active in making their community a place of love and justice, a place where Justice-Love can thrive. I know that's me. Maybe it's you too.

Peter Bridge
May 2024

Introduction

This book is about searching honestly in ourselves and sensitively in our fellow human beings for whatever promotes or blocks Justice-Love. Justice-Love is a robust, demanding kind of love which goes beyond mere feelings. It is a love which moves from human compassion towards tangible healing and reconciliation.

Love is a two-way street. It depends both on what is going on inside us and also what is going on in the "other." Our self-reflection and contemplation open up for us the possibility of growing Justice-Love in ourselves. But the growth of that worthwhile Justice-Love demands that we reflect also, in the most loving way, on what is going on in the "other."

A loving way, yes. But not a vague and indecisive way. We need a plan to guide our reflection and help us stay on track. And we need to commit to the plan and find a way to persevere.

AN ACTION PLAN FOR FINDING JUSTICE-LOVE

In this book you are called back over and over again to three critically important reflections as you search for Justice-Love:

Self-Reflection: Courageously exploring your own situation and truth

Other-Reflection: Unselfishly reflecting on the situation and history of the person/group with whom you hope lovingly to engage, and

Healing/Reconciling Action: Taking steps towards healing, reconciling, loving action.

These steps towards Justice-Love are so crucial that a bit more explanation and a few examples may be helpful.

Self-Reflection: My clergy colleagues and I were privileged to have the late Archbishop Desmond Tutu, Nobel Peace Laureate, as our annual retreat leader several years ago. What a privilege to spend a few days with him! His day did not begin until he had spent a couple of hours in quiet meditation, which was often focused on his gratitude for the love and blessings in his own life. This was clearly the wellspring of the compassionate and courageous love he was able to bring to the most painful situations.

Tutu would be the last one to claim he was just simply a loving person. Where did his courageous love come from? This love that could break through the hard shell of mere self-interest? It came from quiet self-reflection and the openness and wisdom it produces, and his humble heart — which knew its place in the Universe. He understood that each one of us is simultaneously of little significance and of immense significance. He did not consider himself as better or more deserving than anyone else and understood that one's importance comes from a profound connection to all — brother and sister to all, healer of all, lover of all!

Quiet self-reflection is love's seedbed. It is essential for anyone who wants to cultivate a robust healing love. For most of us, this will mean adjusting our routines so that we are less dominated by technology, less seduced by all kinds of media trying to lure us in. What a worthwhile goal...to make room for the love that heals! It is crucial that we cultivate the quiet and stillness that make this possible. The "core questions" at the end of each chapter are designed to help you with this self-reflection.

Other-Reflection: Other-Reflection (or Other-Esteeming) is in direct contrast to what has come to be called "othering." "Othering" is a nasty business! It's a process whereby a person or group highlights the differences between the self and another, or between a group and another group, in a way that suggests the other is somehow "less than," even sometimes less human. It leads to things like racism, sexism, ageism, heterosexism and many other "put-downs" of persons or groups.

A tragic result of "othering" is often hate and polarization in a community or society. But Other-Reflection or Other-Esteeming leads in the opposite direction towards a very positive outcome: mutual understanding, valuing, unity and love. Though I find both "Other-Esteeming" and "Other-Reflection" to be helpful phrases, I will mainly use "Other-Reflection" because it reminds us that, after self-reflection, the process of understanding and caring begins with quiet and humble reflection on another person or group's precious humanity and their current circumstances.

The "I-Thou" relationship described by German-Jewish philosopher Martin Buber (1970) offers a good model of this activity I call "other-reflection." A hundred years ago he dared to imagine people relating to each other in a deep dialogue of love and acceptance. He called this an "I-You" relationship in contrast to an "I-It" relationship in which the other is reduced to a mere object. Though Buber did not originally intend it, "You" was translated as "Thou" in English—a happy decision as it turns out because "Thou" is a word usually reserved for nobility and divinity. It had the effect of affirming even more how special our relationships can be—relationships that so honor others and their realities that only the word "Thou" can do them justice.

In short, the other person is not a mere object to be acted upon in some way. We don't get to set goals for the other person or judge their reality. Rather, in our deep mutual honoring of each other, we open a channel between us that can produce a deeper humanity, a deeper truth, a healing love. Genuine healing love is seeded and then cultivated in a mutual process between persons. Our own self-reflection is an essential part of this process. But so is our respectful non-judgmental reflection on the person or group we aspire to love.

If we have already prejudged a person, put them in a box, then sadly we have put the opportunity for healing on "pause." We can get it going again by reflecting with an open mind and heart on the other person's utterly valuable history and reality. We can put ourselves in their shoes. We can choose to engage in this indispensable reflection about our fellow human beings, their joy, their pain, their fears, oppression they have experienced and may still be experiencing. Or we can stubbornly refuse to open ourselves in this way and block the development of love and reconciliation between us.

I find myself inspired and motivated in my "other-reflections" when I ponder the greeting used by the Zulu people in my native South Africa. "Sawubona" means "I see you." It's a greeting that implies a willingness to linger a while and be truly present to another person — very different from a casual "Hi" as we walk rapidly by.

I spent some time improving my command of *isiZulu*, the Zulu language, at a mission in KwaZulu that happened to be on top of a mountain. The experienced priest-in-charge and I were planning our day of pastoral visits. From the edge of the mountain, we viewed the villages visible in the rolling hills and valleys below. He pointed to two we could visit. I suggested we could manage three or four.

"We'll see," he said. In fact, we were lucky to visit even the second village. Why? Because of "Sawubona." We met many people on the mountain paths along the way. Each meeting was not a passing throwaway greeting. We lingered a while and made the "I see you" greeting true. The getting to know and "see" and serve happened with each encounter.

I shared that story a number of times in talks when I first came to the US. And it has been most gratifying to see and hear it repeated many times over the years in articles or sermons. If only it could inspire us to be more truly present to each other. And deeply reflect on another person's reality.

Another example is the yoga greeting "Namaste," which is sometimes translated "I greet the divine in you." Thought about its meaning is helpful if you are serious about seeing another person as worthy of utter respect. I like to think that Buber would approve because he hinted that the I-Thou relationship could move us in the direction of a kind of participation in the divine.

Reflection on the person or group you aspire to love is essential for a deep healing love to emerge. Core questions at the end of each chapter are designed to help you suspend pre-judgments and open yourself to the full and rich reality of a person or group.

Healing/Reconciling Action: The third step is enacting the love that heals. Out of self-reflection and other-reflection springs loving action.

Tutu's humble self-knowledge combined with deep compassion for other people propelled him to courageous loving action. He risked his safety by physically standing between the threatening apartheid police and the people he was protecting. He spoke truth to power at great risk to himself.

But the treasure of Desmond Tutu is not just what he was able to achieve by way of love. The treasure is also in the way this simple caring human being showed us how that kind of love can take hold and grow in any person.

Most of us won't win the Nobel Peace Prize for our loving action and hopefully that's not our goal. But quiet, consistent self- and other-reflection can nurture in us a reconciling love that motivates loving action. The core questions at the end of each chapter may help nudge you towards loving actions that seem right in your particular circumstances.

The end of each chapter is best thought of as just the *beginning* of your quest for the love that brings reconciliation and healing. That's when your reflection begins in earnest.

In summary, this brief book invites you to embark on a journey of self-reflection and self-discovery about love and justice. It's an opportunity to reflect on yourself in light of the most common impediments to our cultivating a powerful healing love in ourselves and developing the inner resources that can overcome those impediments. We will look at what blocks love and what frees it, how we can cultivate Justice-Love in ourselves, and then reach toward each other with this healing kind of love!

I feel sure you will see yourself in these reflections because we all do. One or another of the "mirrors" may be especially significant at a particular time and place on your journey. For me, the book is a kind of *guidebook* I need to return to from time to time in the ever-changing circumstances of my life. My hope is that it might be that kind of companion for you too!

Each chapter is a mirror aimed at assisting you in finding your particular blocks or strengths in the matter of love. And not just any love. Justice-Love. Love that can heal deep societal hurts.

MAPPING OUT THE JOURNEY TO JUSTICE-LOVE

The Journey:

Chapter 1 helps us to understand the journey we are about to undertake and how our energy will be fueled and refueled by:

- honest self-reflection, and
- our sincere esteeming of other people and groups.

Equipment Needed:

Chapters 2, 3 and 4 help us gather essential equipment:

- a strong sense of our shared humanity as the foundation of Justice-Love
- an attitude of profound respect as we approach our fellow human beings
- a willingness to see another's reality as "sacred space"

Energy Boosters along the Way:

Chapters 5 and 6 offer us important aids to help us persevere in our justice-seeking practice of self- and other-reflection. We are encouraged to cultivate:

- Stillness,
- Mindfulness,
- Wonder, and
- Gratitude.

Common Obstacles:

The remaining chapters highlight common obstacles to the development of Justice-Love. We are invited to focus our self-reflections on them to see if they have relevance to our journey:

- Cultural arrogance
- Isolation
- "Stuckness" in the ways of our original families
- Ungroundedness

- Entrenched anger and defensiveness as a result of trauma
- Elitist, cultural or racist biases
- Reluctance to confront "the powerful"
- Forgiveness without accountability

Conclusion:

We are invited to glance back over the chapter titles, our reflections, any notes we may have made and places where we discovered some significant aspect of our own journey. What blocks us from being active as reconcilers? What work can we continue to do about that? What new insights have empowered us to take courageous healing action? How can we continue to nourish that courage through the crucial inner work of self-reflection and other-esteeming?

Disclaimers

Confidentiality: Confidentiality has been carefully observed in this book. Any pastoral or counseling situations described reflect real situations which actually occurred. But names and circumstances have been altered sufficiently to make any person or group unrecognizable.

Cultural Respect: I have tried to write in a manner that does not privilege my culture over anyone else's. Any failures discovered will be corrected in future editions.

Privilege Acknowledgement: In both my native South Africa and my adopted USA, I have been privileged by a history which includes exploitation and injustice. The very systems from which I benefited were — and still often are — the cause of immense deprivation of my fellow human beings. Acknowledgment of that is just the beginning. It is not enough. I commit to working on the kind of love that reconciles and repairs. Hopefully this book can be a part of that.

1

TREASURE HUNT
Searching for Justice-Love

*"Each day we practice looking deeply into ourselves and into the situation
of our brothers and sisters. It is the most serious work we can do."*
~ Thich Nhat Hanh ~
Living Buddha, Living Christ

The game my children loved most was "Treasure Hunt." At
birthday parties and on other special occasions, it was my job to
create one for them. The children literally squealed with delight as
one hidden clue led them to discover the next hidden clue somewhere
else in the house or the garden. On and on, clue after clue, they
persevered until at last they were led to the treasure itself. But the
game was not without frustrations and whining! "Difficult clues."
"Taking too long."

Searching for Justice-Love can be a bit like that. We start with
great enthusiasm but tire quickly when we meet obstacles both in
ourselves and in those we set out to love.

We are about to set out on a journey of discovery. We're going to
search in ourselves and in our fellow human beings for the makings
of the greatest treasure of all—Justice-Love, love that can heal
relationships, communities, and even larger conflicts in our world.
Hopefully, as with the children's treasure hunt, there will be squeals
of delight along the way. But the journey will sometimes be arduous.
Finding and then cultivating healing love is hard work. Digging for
clues will sometimes be frustrating and feel unproductive.

In today's world, many factors have combined to hide—and even
bury—the most authentic forms of love. We are left puzzled and

1

confused. Is *this* really love? Is *that* really love? This really feels good and wholesome. Surely it must be the real thing!

The meaning of love has been blunted and obscured. Overly romantic and sentimental ideas of love make it seem like its core strength consists in feeling and passion instead of in caring action. Love often comes across as a passive quality — as if love just happens if you're good or lucky. Suggestions that we "be more loving" can leave us puzzled about love's meaning and frustrated in our confused attempts to make it happen. What *is* this love? Just when we think we understand it, it seems to slip away.

The entertainment industry often paints pictures of love as romantic — springing naturally from the heart. Religions talk up a storm about love but do little to define it or highlight how costly and precious it is in terms of self-honesty and accountability.

These factors contribute to confusion about the meaning of love. That is why stillness and self-reflection are so important in the search for Justice-Love. They can help remove the blocks that so often get in the way. They can clear the way for self-honesty and motivate us to explore another person's reality.

From a thousand clumsy encounters — my own and those shared with me by others — I know that love can be very messy. It reminds me of an artist's palette. The palette may be messy but the masterpiece is still compelling and desirable, still worth doing. But it won't paint itself. We have to pick up the brush and get to work.

Sometimes the search goes quite smoothly and we are delighted and energized. When playing the Treasure Hunt game, our children began to understand that some of the most helpful clues were often right under their noses. Hidden in plain sight. This is a lesson we must learn in our search for Justice-Love — that it is not in faraway places but right under our noses in the ordinary encounters of daily life.

Not long after I started in clinical practice, I was assigned a client who needed a wheelchair to get around. Typical of those days, the clinic was not very accessible. When I mentioned on the phone that there would be a couple of steps and heavy doors to negotiate, he said, "We'll be OK."

I wasn't so sure. In fact, I was rather nervous about my part in that "we." Would I know what to do? How much should I help? When should I back off? I was clumsy, but we managed.

"You probably noticed my nervousness and confusion," I said."Would you help me understand how I can assist in a way that is both helpful and comfortable for you?"

Looking relieved, my client smiled. "Thank you!" he said. "Thank you for asking. That already makes me feel helped. Few people ever ask. I can tell that they are uncomfortable and shy but they never ask, so it just makes it worse."

I had just received one of the most important lessons about love. *Get in touch with your own stuff because it affects how you relate to someone else.* Then work to understand the other person's situation and their feelings and needs. Ask, listen, learn!

Sometimes the search for Justice-Love does not go smoothly but is even more productive. We need to be ready for frustration. Being held accountable for our own lazy searching, our tendency to give up, our sometimes willful blindness, can be disheartening. We may be tempted to give up the search.

I once asked a Black colleague in South Africa what the single most important thing was that I, as a white South African, should be doing to be effective in fighting against the injustice of apartheid. He said, "Maybe stop asking me to come up with answers for a problem you whites created."

It felt like a slap in the face. But it was not. I was being held accountable for the smugness and perceived generosity behind my question. Rather than focus on my hurt and embarrassment, I needed to see his reaction as a signpost pointing the way to the next clue in the treasure hunt for Justice-Love. In this case, the clue, if I paid attention, was that I needed to open a way for Justice-Love by looking deeply into my colleague's situation and trying to understand the feelings underlying *his* challenging response. *His* feelings, not mine.

Our treasure hunt is similar to the work of archaeologists. They are extremely sensitive and careful as they uncover precious artifacts of history. They patiently brush away whatever is hiding history's important lessons. What a great model for our important search for Justice-Love! We need to cultivate that kind of sensitivity as we try to understand the often painful feelings and histories of people we aspire to love.

The stakes are high. Justice-love can be a powerful force for healing and each of us is a potential generator of that powerful force. Healing and reconciliation have never been needed more than they are today. Let's get searching.

Self-Reflection: What is your gut reaction to the suggestion that developing Justice-Love may require of you some deep inner searching? What could you do to create for yourself an atmosphere of stillness and self-reflection? Fewer "good reads" about justice and more quiet reflection? Could this be especially important for you in your search for Justice-Love? The self-reflection is the most important part.

Other-Reflection: Remember Buber's "I-Thou" perspective? Think of the other person (or each person in a group) as "Thou," a wonderful human being worthy of your utmost respect.

Perhaps the idea of reflecting/meditating on the feelings and needs of another person or group is new to you. If so, it may take quite a bit of practice. But there's no time like the present to get started. Would you put aside a few minutes and dive right in today? Choose a person or group and ask yourself how much you really know about their history and circumstances.

Healing/Reconciling Action: Read through the Introduction one more time before going further. The idea of Justice-Love growing out of "deep looking" into yourself and into the situation of another person or group is so crucial that it may be helpful to get it even more clearly in focus. Are there some concrete actions, however small, you might take today that will help you get to understand a little better the pain of a group you want to love?

Have you read books that reinforce mere knowledge about justice without motivating any action? Are you making time for quiet moments that could set your heart on fire and energize your action? Is some "intellectual decluttering" called for so you can make room for stillness and reflection that leads to loving action?

2

FIRST, WE ARE HUMAN
Love's Original Family

"Compassion becomes real when we recognize our shared humanity."
~ Pema Chödrön ~

What a privilege to have been born in Africa and to have spent much of my life there! I experienced first hand one of Africa's great treasures: "Ubuntu."

Its meaning is summed up in the words of this African proverb: *"A person is a person through other persons."* or *"I am because you are!"* (Ngomane, 2020) It refers to the deepest connection of human beings to each other.

This wisdom is found also in the Buddhist teaching that nothing can "be" by itself. Everything in the cosmos must "inter-be" with everything else. There is such wisdom across all cultures about our shared humanity, our "inter-being." But human beings too often forget this. We impoverish ourselves when we turn away from this treasured wisdom.

I have found it useful to pair "ubuntu" with the simple Zulu greeting I mentioned earlier: "Sawubona" or "I see you." I link them together because "ubuntu" remains a proverb, an aspiration, an ideal, unless we do the work to really "see" human beings in front of us. Ubuntu can be a healing way of living and loving but it doesn't just magically happen. The beginning of deep human connection and understanding is to truly "see" the immensely valuable human person in your presence. "Sawubona, I see you!" And the response: "Yebo, Sawubona. Yes, I see you too!"

Wouldn't it be wonderful if we could linger a while and "see" each other more? If our "seeing" was a reflection of our "inter-being" and our valuing of our shared humanity? What if we could see past the merely technical or useful to the inherent value of a fellow human being standing right in front of us—reaching beyond faults and foibles, beyond what may seem unattractive—to the humanity we share and can value together?

Our relating to each other is sometimes based too much on our personal agenda. We have needs of others and sometimes manipulate them to get those needs met. We could do with a lot more of the "I-Thou" kind of relating, in which we see another not as an "it" but as a "Thou." Seeing another as "Thou" prepares us to be respectful in our attitudes and actions. We honor and try to understand a person's own sacred reality without imposing ours. Sociologist Holly Oxhandler (2022) tells us that the Yoga greeting "Namaste" literally means "bowing to you," which in itself connotes respect. I embrace the even deeper respect that has come to be associated with the Namaste greeting: "The sacred in me recognizes the sacred in you!"

What's the point of all this? "Ubuntu," "Inter-being," "I-Thou?" That first of all we need to recognize our shared humanity. That it is in the context of our shared humanity that Justice-Love can take root and thrive. If we want to cultivate Justice-Love in ourselves, and reach out to others with Justice-Love, then a high priority for us must be genuine valuing of our shared humanity. Shared humanity is love's "first family." We need to live and love within that family.

How do we do that? How do we live in the spirit of "ubuntu"? How do we hold onto the awareness that we are interconnected and dependent on each other? The awareness that our Justice-Love for each other starts with an understanding of our inter-being with each other?

Self-reflection and reflection on the situation of our fellow human beings is an important first step. We live in a culture which too often deceives us into thinking that "power over," "difference from," and the "accumulation of things" will make us feel better than our fellow human-beings. Mostly it just exaggerates competitiveness with each other and makes us forget each other's inherent worth as human beings. Counteracting those strong cultural messages requires the personal humility and deep caring that comes with honest reflection. Reflection may seem quiet and ineffectual in a loud and materialistic culture like ours. But I know of nothing more effective in increasing our awareness of our shared humanity.

Self-Reflection: It isn't always easy to live in the spirit of "ubuntu." Are you aware of or do you need to increase your awareness of attitudes or actions in yourself that stress "difference from" rather than "inter-being with" your fellow human-beings? You may find it helpful to think about a particular person or group as you think about what enhances your sense of human connection — and also what may be dulling that sense. Feeling better than? Having goals for? Needing to be accorded special recognition? Enjoying it a bit too much when you are already being treated with great respect? Assuming you know all you need to know about someone to understand their needs? These are the kinds of things that interfere with a humble recognition that we share a common humanity.

Other-Reflection: Think of the other person (or each person in a group) as "Thou," a wonderful human being worthy of your utmost respect.

Looking deeply into the circumstances and history of another person or group is never easy. It requires us to suspend our judgments and assumptions. Are you good at that? Are you good at thinking of another person as "Thou," an utterly valuable human-being deserving of your respect? Most of us aren't.

Envision someone or some group with whom you would like to improve your relationship. It may be especially helpful to think about a person or group often looked down on in your community. Then think about what makes that challenging for you and what adjustments of your attitude might smooth the way.

Healing/Reconciling Action: Practice engaging in a new way with the people you encounter in your daily life. Your envisioning of a person as utterly worthy of your respect may have empowered you to act in a more respectful way toward them. Perhaps you are ready to try some new approaches. There's no time like the present!

3

THE HOLY OF HOLIES
Love Pauses and Prepares

"This is the Holy of Holies."
~ Ezekiel 41:4 (JPS Tanakh, 1985) ~

Justice-Love doesn't just happen. We need to prepare ourselves carefully if our goal is to love with a passion for justice. If we're serious about cultivating a reverent "Thou" attitude then we need to take appropriate steps to prepare for the encounter.

One of my earliest professors loved to use the example of the high priest in the Hebrew Bible. It always surprised me because he was teaching a "secular" clinical course. But I got the message and have never forgotten it.

"Before the high priest could enter the Holy of Holies," said the professor, "he had to go through several stringent preparatory steps. This was to induce in himself the humility and awe appropriate for one about to enter a sacred place." Not a bad meditation for us when we are about to have access to a person's private and often fragile world. A tender world which merits the description "holy of holies!"

"The most important thing you can do as you prepare for your next client," our professor would also say, "is to remember that you are about to be allowed into a tender holy place. The rest of your training can fall into place after that."

What a great message for all of us who aspire to love with Justice-Love. We want to love in a way that heals, restores, reconciles. It all starts with attention and respect. But if we're not careful, our busy lives full of distractions can wreak havoc on our loving "presence." Our busy agendas tend to cling to us as we enter another person's "holy of holies." That makes it hard for us to achieve an attentive presence. We need to gather ourselves into the sacred present moment. To come back from wherever we have gone so that we can truly "be there" for a person or group.

When I arrived for a quiet retreat some years ago, the retreat director caught me off guard. "What have you brought with you?" he asked.

"Oh, just a couple of tapes and an article or two," I said.

"Would you mind being a bit more specific?"

I thought for a moment. "Next week's sermon outline and an article that may help me with that. A seminarian's paper I need to give feedback on. Agenda and notes for the food pantry meeting that is scheduled for the night I get back. Just things related to spirituality."

The director held me in his gaze. "Would you consider locking all that stuff in the trunk of your car for the next couple of days?"

Ouch! He was quite right, of course. Even so, I had to force myself to drag those distractions back to my car. But it made for a particularly rewarding retreat. It reinforced for me the truth about how easily we can deceive ourselves about what's really important.

Mindfulness—being truly present in the present moment—is much talked about these days. Being present not in the past or the future but right here, right now. This kind of mindful presence is essential for entering the "holy of holies" of another person or group's reality. Mindfulness helps us tame our wandering minds so that we are more able to focus on the one we want to love.

However, mindfulness is not easy to achieve. Here's an exercise that helps build on small successes.

Think of each time you are able truly to inhabit the present moment as a precious jewel—for yourself and for those you love. Pretend you are making a bracelet. Each time you successfully "capture" and dwell in the moment, even for a brief while, add a jewel to the bracelet. At the end of a day, you may think your bracelet is rather scraggly. But even one or two jewels represent the great value of your living mindfully.

With time, you will sometimes be able to make a full bracelet. And maybe one day a lovely necklace! As your mindfulness increases, your compassion and presence as a lover and healer will deepen — and those you seek to love fully will benefit.

You've tried mindfulness or something similar and your resolution only lasts a day or so? Has it been difficult for you to be consistent with it? Join the club. Our culture gets more distracting by the day. Not much prepares us for this kind of nurturing stillness.

Our personal "rituals" of preparation will differ because each of us is different. Different things calm you and bring you to a state of presence. Think of something that worked to calm you in the past. If you feel discouraged, focus on your goal: Justice-Love — the love that can make the world a better place!

We aspire to bring a reconciliatory love to people who are hurting, people who are oppressed. If we're serious about entering the "holy of holies" of their precious selves, we must prepare respectfully.

Self-Reflection: How vulnerable am I to the culture's relentless pulling me away from the precious present moment? Does it affect my ability to enter another's world with great respect? In what situations? Are you ready to learn? Ready to love? Consider how you may need to prepare yourself to be a respectful listener and learner.

Other-Reflection: Think of the other person (or each person in a group) as "Thou," a wonderful human being worthy of your utmost respect.

Bear with me as I remind you again and again about developing a deep respect for your fellow human beings. "Other-esteeming," "Thou-ing," is a new behavior for too many of us!

How well do you know the person or group you aspire to love? What do you know of their particular histories of pain, loss, deprivation? Have you tried to get a sense of the way in which their unique experiences may have made them suspicious or even fearful of you? As you stand at the threshold of relationship, what might they be feeling or experiencing that requires special care and respect?

Healing/Reconciling Action: Do a relentless and honest assessment of the things that stop you from being truly present to yourself and others. Draw up a plan of action for modifying or eliminating these and commit to it. But make it realistic and doable for you. Take small steps to increase the likelihood of little successes that may spur you on to bigger changes.

4

HOLY GROUND
Love Takes Off Its Shoes

"Take off your shoes: you are in the sacred valley..."
~ Qur'an 20:12 ~

We've stressed the importance of preparation before we cross the threshold into another human being's sacred space. Preparing to enter the holy of holies is just the beginning. Respect is just as important once we are inside.

There is a mosque just walking distance from my home and I learn so much when I sometimes join my Muslim sisters and brothers for Friday prayers. I am always touched and educated by the custom of removing our shoes before taking our place in the sacred worship space. It's a constant reminder to me that I need to "remove my shoes" — suspend my assumptions and judgments when I am "invited in" by someone. I need to adjust my attitude and prepare for a human encounter in the same way as I might prepare for a divine encounter.

When we visited our son after he had married and established his new home, we were shocked when he asked us to take off our shoes. This had not been the custom in our home, and besides, this was the son we had to cajole into cleaning his room! We complied, of course, but not without a few chuckles in the car when we left.

Most cultures across the world have an unwritten rule that your home is your castle and you get to make the rules. And for the most part, people accept that. But it is more challenging when the "home" being talked about is the internal essence of a person's humanity with all its history, heartbreaks and joys, foibles and fears.

We forget that they are allowed to make their own rules about that "home" too. Having removed our shoes we need to keep them off, and do everything in our power to preserve and protect their holy ground for the nurturing of healing love.

Protecting someone's "holy ground" is about observing "boundaries." In recent years, there has been an increased emphasis on the importance of observing appropriate "boundaries" in relationships. Crossing over the boundary into someone's space through power or manipulative persuasion makes it difficult or impossible for the person to feel safe and protected.

Do you like people to tidy up when you visit? I'm torn. A terrible mess with not even a chair to sit on can seem a bit disrespectful to visitors. At the same time, a comfortable lived-in kind of untidiness makes me feel like a trusted friend. If we seek justice and reconciliation, the "home" of someone's private life or a group's guarded culture needs to be given generous tolerance when it comes to the matter of how tidy it is. Someone's private space may not look "tidy" to you but it is holy ground to them.

No matter what, take off your shoes. Without reflection, you may see only a "mess," based on your unthinking definition of "tidy." But what you dismiss as a mess may be the result of pain and rage, of unresolved oppression. When we treat the "messes" of others with respect, we lay the groundwork for mutual efforts toward Justice-Love.

Without careful reflection, we can carelessly violate another's boundary. Boundary violations set back our efforts to improve relationships, whereas calm reflection can prepare us to be with someone in their pain and rage without assuming we can enter their holy ground. Uninvited crossing of the boundary induces defensiveness in people you want to love.

Professional helpers have "external" controls— such as regulations and supervision—to help them recognize and preserve the boundaries of those they work with. But most of us seeking to improve our personal relationships must rely on our own "internal" controls, enhanced by our self- and other- reflection. Honest self-reflection helps us curb our rush to enter private space when it is based on our need or personal agendas — and not in the interest of guarding the holy ground of another. Our careful reflection on that holy ground — the circumstances, the needs, the sacred life of another person, invokes those "internal controls" that prepare us to be respectful when we are invited in.

A deep respect for boundaries leads to good outcomes and sometimes surprising breakthroughs.

A bad accident rendered homebound a severely depressed woman at a critical moment in her therapy. She asked if I could continue her weekly sessions at her home. I consulted my supervisor and the head of our agency and was given the go-ahead. I arranged for appropriate boundaries and resumed her therapy. What might have been a setback to the therapy was transformed into a considerable advantage because the care with which we approached maintaining her boundaries preserved the client's sense of emotional safety.

An angry young teen was having a hard time bonding with me and trusting the process of therapy. He was passionate about dirt-biking. One day he arrived and practically ordered me to come down to the parking lot, and I did. He showed me some of his tricks and explained the ins and outs of his cherished hobby. In effect, he invited me into his holy space. I learned much about what was important to him.

He never asked again for this kind of exception to our normal process and in the next session, we returned to the usual business of therapy. But there was a breakthrough in his trust of me and the beginnings of important progress for him. He had invited me into his "holy" space and I had responded with respect, and then returned to our appropriate formal boundaries.

And what about the larger groups we aspire to love? Groups in whose healing process we would like to share. Are boundaries important in larger groups too? Absolutely!

An anti-apartheid group I belonged to brought Blacks and whites together, at some risk, because in the apartheid system it was illegal. I remember feeling a bit smug and self-satisfied about my involvement in this important struggle. Pressing my point about some action I thought we should take, I was firmly put in my place by a Black member of the group: "Peter, this is our Black struggle, not your white struggle!"

This too was a matter of love and a matter of boundaries. I felt I had something to offer but I needed to check my self-importance at the door and respectfully "take off my shoes." My attitude needed to be one of learning in what ways my walking side-by-side in this struggle might be experienced as helpful and loving. A bit of self-reflection on my part was called for.

After a 7000-mile journey I arrived at university to find some influential students wanted me to be sent packing. "What is our school doing admitting a white South African in the midst of all the oppression of Blacks going on in South Africa!?"

Calm reflection was not my first reaction. I was shocked, angry and defensive. In large part, my selection for the scholarship was based on my solidarity with those involved in the anti-apartheid struggle. However, when I calmed down and was able to reflect, I had some important insights. Whatever solidarity I had with Blacks in South Africa paled into insignificance when compared with the bond forged in shared oppression that American Blacks shared with South African Blacks — even from thousands of miles away.

What has all this got to do with boundaries?! Without even realizing it, I had crossed a boundary into a local situation of which I had little understanding. I had not reflected much on the special solidarity Blacks in the US had with those being oppressed in South Africa. Some experienced my presence as insulting and invasive.

Others ventured into my space and felt my presence could be useful and foster understanding. In a difficult situation that could have turned adversarial, there was enough mutual "removing of the shoes" on both sides that healing and growth could occur. Just a few months later the Black professor who facilitated our anti-racism seminar asked me to co-lead it with her.

Boundaries are not always perfectly clear. They often overlap in confusing ways based on a person or group's distinctive experiences and sensitivities. This makes it even more important to reflect humbly on our own situation and lovingly on the reality of the person or group we claim to care about.

Respect for boundaries is an early and essential step on the way to loving justly. The metaphor of "removing one's shoes" to respect sacred space is especially important with larger groups and even whole cultures. Reflection makes us more likely to check at the door our arrogant assumptions about what we have to offer and what others "need."

Entering the "holy of holies" is just the beginning. Once we are trusted to enter someone's holy ground, the respect needs to continue! Having removed our shoes, we need to keep them off, and do everything in our power to preserve and protect that holy ground for the nurturing of healing love.

Self-Reflection: When reaching out to people who are angry, afraid, vulnerable, are you able to notice what's going on inside you? Need recognition for your efforts? Feel defensive if you seem to be rejected? Reflect on some of the examples that have been given and imagine what might have been going on in you? Do some self-reflection about a situation you are currently dealing with.

Any insights about your needs, motivation, feelings? In your most honest self-review, are you aware of times when your healing effort has been thwarted by the emergence of your own self-importance or other personal gratification? If so, don't put yourself down. Instead try to understand what thoughts and attitudes might affect your ability to offer healing love to a person or group. And what different attitudes might prepare you better.

Other-Reflection: Think of the other person (or each person in a group) as "Thou," a wonderful human being worthy of your utmost respect.

Is there a person or group you aspire to love but know very little about? What might make them scared, vulnerable, suspicious of your intentions? Can you try hard to imagine what might make them especially in need of your efforts to understand and provide safety? Have you tried to help others and been disappointed by their reactions? What do you think they may have been feeling? Could they have been put off by something in your approach?

Healing/Reconciling Action: Identify a couple of situations in which you will begin the process of creating respect and safety between yourself and another person or group. How might you go about that based on your reflection on the other person's or group's needs? Take the first steps.

5

BE STILL AND KNOW
Love's Quiet Nursery

"Be still and know…"
~ Psalm 46 (NRSV) ~

" B e still and know_____"
Fill in the blank. One of my favorite scripture texts is: "Be still and know that I am God!" from Psalm 46. It brings me back from fruitless worries and distractions to a place of calm and truth. The reason I say "fill in the blank" is that not everyone is comfortable with a reference to God. And to do its work, the text doesn't require that. Try any of these: Be still and know…your truth, your priorities, what is really important. Be still and know…the wonder of your existence. Be still so that you can look around you and truly experience the wonders of nature and your part in it. Be still and better understand what's going on inside you right this moment. Be still, be still, be still! Make it a mantra of sorts — something that brings you back to what's really important and valuable.

Jane and I have a marvelous old Buddhist gong that serves a similar purpose in our relationship. If one of us, or sometimes both of us, seems to be going a bit nuts with worry, blowing something up out of all proportion or just simply getting off track from what we know to be our chosen shared values, the other will gently ring the gong. Because of the meaning we have long attached to this little ritual, it brings us back to a better place, a better attitude. Very similar to "Be still and know…"

The cultivation of deep substantive love, the kind that brings healing to ourselves, our relationships and our world, needs quiet reflection and contemplation. I can't tell you exactly how you should do that. There are so many variations these days, all claiming to be the exact right method. I urge you to find the approach that helps you to be still and step aside from the relentless seduction of our noisy culture. The kind of love that really matters, that is willing to be unselfishly active in service of a loved one, has a hard time competing with a culture that has become expert at the seduction of our minds and hearts.

I can't stress this enough. If we aspire to be healers, or if we are already in that role but want to be better at it, regularly being quiet and contemplative is not just a choice. It must be an essential part of our lives. Noise and mind-clutter (TV on all the time, checking phone constantly, always looking at some screen) have become so much a part of us that we no longer realize that they are a problem.

If you used to be a lot better at countering the relentless distractions, then you may want to take a look at what exactly happened to change that. If you feel just fine with the relentless "noise" in your life and don't know what all the fuss is about, you may want to think about the things you are missing. Among them may be exciting possibilities, personal connections, growth opportunities — things that may now have disappeared from your environment because of the pervasiveness of the "same-old, same-old" passive entertainment or constant engagement with a screen. Cell phones, internet communications, social media have become a problem even for people who think of themselves as mature and responsible in their use of these resources.

We need to develop the ability to laugh at ourselves for the way we have fallen into this trap and have a bit of humility about it, but then proceed to get serious about some adjustments in our own lives. There is something ironic about adults who started off by distancing themselves from any possibility that they, in all their maturity, could possibly become dominated by these gadgets. "How terrible that people are so hooked and have to have their phones with them at every moment," they said. "And how awful about our kids constantly in front of a screen. We've got to do something about it!"

But now here we are, nearly every last one of us, just as seduced by instant tech as any young person might be. Just as enslaved by the cunning lords of the industry and their marketing cohorts.

Effective healing love proceeds out of stillness—the stillness that breeds self-honesty, humility, an atmosphere of calm—and the flexibility that is needed in our messy ever-changing lives. This stillness anchors and positions us to offer love in the messiness and conflict of personal, family, community or even larger national or global contexts. Calm self-reflective healers are needed.

"Be still and know…"

———

Self-Reflection: Even if you no longer have, or never had, any interest in formal religion or spiritual practices, spend some time pondering the wisdom and benefit of some age-old practices. A day of rest? Some quiet reflection time each day? An occasional retreat from the hustle and bustle of life to reflect on your values and meaning in your life. Try not to fight against the universal and age-old wisdom in these pursuits. Instead try to acknowledge that our frenzied culture is missing something, and you may be too.

Other-Reflection: Think of the other person (or each person in a group) as "Thou," a wonderful human being worthy of your utmost respect.

Without judgment, ponder with love and compassion the way people you care about are overwhelmed and trapped by a culture that is hell bent on capturing their allegiance for marketing or other purposes. Be compassionate too when you ponder the fact that so many people struggling just to survive have little opportunity to "Be still and know..." The push and pull of the daily grind may come across as so much noise. That's a great reminder that our reaching out to those we want to love is most effective when it is quiet and respectful—and does not come across as just one more noisy demand.

Healing/Reconciling Action: What adjustments can you make in your own life to make room for more time to "Be Still And Know..."? What healing might you do through modeling? Or through a gentle invitation to nudge people away from a noisy and distracting atmosphere toward one that is calming and nurturing?

Your invitation to someone to go on a quiet walk may be more welcome than you at first think. There is a healing touch to shared silence or quiet togetherness. Taking the initiative to arrange a retreat for a group involved in conflict can have a similar healing effect. Be creative in helping yourself and your community move towards a more calming and healing atmosphere.

6

AWE AND GRATITUDE
Love's Wellsprings

"The more I wonder, the more I love."
~ Alice Walker, *The Color Purple* ~

Awe and gratitude are the wellsprings of compassion and love — essential attitudes for the cultivation of the love that can heal and reconcile and make the world a better place. They encourage a quiet and constant attention to the magnificent mystery of life.

Unfortunately for us, and for those whose lives we touch, we are too often oblivious to the sacred mystery of which we are a part. And yet it is attention to that profound mystery, our embrace of the wonder of life, that generates in us the gratitude that brings forth compassion and love.

How do we get this sense of awe and deep gratitude that produces the healing love our world so needs? Sometimes I see my neighbor, who is an amateur astronomer, gazing at the sky through a huge telescope. He has become very knowledgeable about astronomy. But for him, science gives way to wonder. He is fortunate to have found a way through the maze of mundane concerns to experience wonder and awe at the mystery of the Universe.

Over the course of my career, I have offered an "existential awe" exercise. The exercise goes like this: Get quiet and comfortable and close your eyes. Be aware of your breathing, trying your best to make it slow and deep. Put aside any "easy" answers about your existence that your faith or past philosophy may have required you to hold. Putting aside the easy answers enables you to come face to face with the sheer wonder of existence. Now, try your best to hold on to just this one main thought or curiosity: "I am here, I am alive, I am me. How on earth did this happen?"

The first couple of times, it may be difficult to get into the spirit of this exercise. It's hard to get rid of distractions. It's hard to clear your mind of the answers and assumptions of the past. When these difficulties arise, drop it for the moment. But keep trying. It is so worthwhile. So often I have seen this simple exercise uncover the spring, the trickle, which becomes the river of awe and wonder that is missing in a person's life, the river of awe and wonder that flows powerfully toward gratitude, compassion and love.

Experiences of wonder at the mystery of our existence can produce in us feelings of deep gratitude. But the hurried world we live in makes it hard for us to hold onto them. We live in a complicated web of daily transactions. Most of them reduce thankfulness to shallow feelings of relief that we received something we needed for our safety, survival or perhaps just our enjoyment. Carefully examined, our thankfulness often amounts to a kind of payment of a debt out of good manners or out of the need to remain in good standing with our benefactor or service provider.

Believers may rush to prayers of thanksgiving or even dedicate their lives to caring for others in return for the gift they believe has been given by God but, in the end, even they must come to terms with the fact that the gift of existence itself is not something one can pay back. It is profound! It is earth-shattering! It is humbling! Awe makes us better able to see our proper place in the universe.

We're not talking here about the "Thank You" of good manners or the gratitude that grows out of a sense of mutual indebtedness. We're not talking about thank-you letters or favors granted that make us feel we owe something in return. These have their place — certainly we need more good manners in our society. But the gratitude I'm talking about can perhaps open us to a much deeper kind — gratitude which has a lot to do with developing healing love. Gratitude that springs from our very existence. Gratitude that generates compassion and love is a deep inner response to a gift that cannot be reciprocated.

It's important that we take this gratitude business further than just good manners or an individual spiritual discipline. Though they are important and helpful, thankfulness can easily get bogged down in what is merely conventional. Much of our so-called "civilized" world is embedded in the kind of thankfulness that our parents taught us because certain things are just "done" and other things are simply "not done"!

That is fine as far as it goes but a lot of the time, without even being aware of it, we practice that kind of thankfulness because it would look pretty boorish not to! Likewise a lot of the thankfulness we practice in our "need to get ahead" world is "quid pro quo" thankfulness. I show my thankfulness for something good you did for me by doing something good for you. Quid pro Quo. Tit for tat. This for that.

But this gratitude quest is much more challenging. The gift of life is a gift for which there is no easy "thank you." Our awe and wonder at our very existence help us to know our place and make us want to share our joy with others. And that's the beginning of healing love.

It's important to acknowledge the special difficulties encountered by those who suffer or have suffered abuse, depression or oppression. Suggestions to be grateful can sound hollow in the midst of such suffering. Deep awe and gratitude can co-exist with rage and despair, but we should not take it for granted that people can easily experience them.

Our reflection on the history and present circumstances of people we aspire to love can help us develop a sensitivity to their needs and stop us from making assumptions about their feelings. On the other hand, a careful, respectful approach may open up a place where the sharing of wonder and gratitude paves the way for healing.

The stakes are high. We are trying to develop the kind of love that can heal broken relationships and a hurting world. Awe and gratitude can lead us to that kind of healing. And they're often closer than we think!

Let's open ourselves to wonder and gratitude and seek them out. If we do, compassion and healing love won't be far behind.

———

Self-Reflection: Clear your mind of easy answers to the question "Where have I come from? How on earth did I get here?" Be enveloped by the sheer wonder of it. The magnificent gift of life!

Other-Reflection: Think of the other person (or each person in a group) as "Thou," a wonderful human being worthy of your utmost respect.

As you try to understand the full reality of a person you wish to love, ask yourself what circumstances of their life might inhibit their ability to feel grateful. Be ready to understand their circumstances at as deep a level as you can. To be with them in that difficult place can pave the way for a future moment when together you can plant the seeds of deep gratitude and open a channel of love between the two of you.

Healing/Reconciling Action: Reach out to a person whose seeming lack of gratitude puts you off. Practice being there for them rather than judging. Be alert for opportunities when you may be able to take your relationship deeper even though the initial steps may seem very small.

7

CULTURAL HUMILITY
Setting Love Free

*"A genuine spiritual life is a continuous, daily
striving for freedom and liberation."*
~ Albert Nolan, *Biblical Spirituality* ~

A huge part of the "liberation" mentioned in the quote above is liberation from being stuck within the narrow limits of our own culture. That stuckness often goes hand in hand with a sense that our own culture is better than all other cultures. When we are unable or unwilling to see the value of other cultures and groups, our ability to love them is severely limited. Love gets stuck—imprisoned in a sense of its own superiority and importance. And Love needs to be set free if it is to grow into Justice-Love.

If we *are* able to free ourselves from the stuckness and see our culture in a new light, we can delight in previously undiscovered beauty and correct faults revealed by that light. But cultural stuckness can be hard to recognize and the inability to recognize our stuckness is often the insidious precursor to many forms of unacknowledged but very real systemic injustice.

Some people find it relatively easy to move beyond the limits of their own culture. They welcome the opportunity. Contact with different cultures feels refreshing and energizing. They enjoy new perspectives and experiences and feel enriched by them.

For others wandering out of their own culture is a daunting process. The "unknown" of other cultures feels scary. Sometimes they fear that a new culture will push aside the cherished riches of their own.

If we want to foster Justice-Love in ourselves and between cultures, self- and other-reflection are crucially important. We need to look deeply into ourselves to discover our own often-buried negative attitudes toward other cultures. Our fears and negative attitudes often inhibit the growth of love in us. We need to look deeply into the situations and histories of other people or groups to try to understand *their* fears. Our esteeming of others asks of us an attitude of listening and learning rather than accusing and lecturing. Such an approach is even more important when fear has resulted in defensiveness and sometimes arrogance.

Individuals, groups and even nations can behave in arrogant and over-entitled ways. Perhaps, in individuals, a sense of inflated entitlement is the result of overindulged childhoods. Some individuals or groups may attribute their "success" solely to meritorious hard work and the presence of good fortune in their success is underplayed. Even whole nations sometimes wallow in a sense of over-entitlement and superiority over other countries.

Some in the US seem to conflate patriotism and love of their country with the idea that America can do no wrong — and refuse even to look at the possibility that certain groups have been marginalized, barred from participation in the bounties and opportunities our country has made available to us. Cultural arrogance follows easily from this perception. And Justice-Love is imprisoned as a result.

Unacknowledged "white privilege" is an example of cultural arrogance. At its core, the phrase simply asks white people to think about ways in which their culture and upbringing may have given them social and economic advantages that non-white individuals have not enjoyed in the past or do not now enjoy.

As a white South African, I was born and grew up into a very comfortable existence but had almost no awareness of my privileged status. I was simply "in" it. I knew nothing different. When I was settling into the "bubble" of my white boarding school in the 1950s, I had no idea that the architects of apartheid were busy passing laws to ensure a lower standard of education for Blacks. I matriculated eight years later with what was called a "3rd Class Matric." It just barely qualified me to enter university. But I could choose that path if I wanted it.

I still gave little or no thought to the way in which my schooling and the "white" system of education gave me huge advantages over Black South Africans. It took a few more years for the light bulb to go off! Part of my first assignment as a priest was to teach in a high school. I had no training and no clue! Fortunately the highly-gifted Black teachers showed me the ropes. They also shared the struggles and setbacks they had experienced in the inferior Black educational system to eventually achieve the status of qualified teacher.

Why do I share this story? In apartheid South Africa where the privileged status of whites was crystal clear, we whites still easily missed it or chose to ignore it. We were just "in" it! How easily that can happen anywhere, especially when the "privilege" hides in a long-standing tradition of rugged individualism and the direction to "Pull yourself up by the bootstraps." The idea that everyone should just "pull themselves up by their own bootstraps" blocks attention to the fact that some "bootstraps" are easier to pull up than others. Some families have the advantage of sufficient means and an ethnicity that has experienced little, if any, discrimination or injustice. Others do not enjoy those advantages.

Unfortunately, the suggestion that white privilege may be at play is often greeted with denial, defensiveness, anger and arrogance. "How dare you even suggest such a thing!" When a whole group of people has that attitude, individual arrogance rises to a level of cultural arrogance. And cultural arrogance interferes with the development of the love that can heal division.

The phrase "cultural humility" was first coined by Melanie Tervalon and Jann Murray-Garcia (1998). Cultural humility is an attitude of humility about one's own particular context and culture — an attitude that recognizes its limitations and flaws. If we have cultural humility, we continue to honor and celebrate the good things about our histories and cultures but are open to deep and honest examination of negative aspects of which we have been unaware—those which have inhibited us from learning about and honoring other cultures. When we are ready to diagnose and shed our cultural stuckness, love is set free—and reconciliation can finally and fully begin.

Self-Reflection: Is there something that you are holding onto much too tightly out of a sense of pride, defensiveness, fear of someone's judgment? Are you stuck in a position which is making it hard for you to experience some inner change and liberation? Is it perhaps a cultural issue? Are you "in" your culture in such a way that it is inhibiting you from the fresh air and rich learning offered to you by opening yourself to others?

Other-Reflection: Think of the other person (or each person in a group) as "Thou," a wonderful human being worthy of your utmost respect.

Today, try with a generous heart to identify a person or group you have largely closed yourself off from. A person or group that your reflection has helped you realize you know hardly anything about. A person or group perhaps that in the past you have dismissed and not really listened to because you assumed you knew better or had nothing to learn from them. Seek out a book or resource that would educate you about that person or group's reality.

Are you perhaps a privileged traveler? One who has the means to take a vacation at a destination where great luxury exists next to great poverty? There are few places you can go for a luxury vacation these days where the luxury you enjoy does not come as a result of either past or current exploitation of others. Would you be willing to spend even just a little bit of such a vacation focusing on and esteeming those persons around you whose history of pain, or whose current struggle, is contributing to your happy place in the sun? That's the kind of shift in our attitude that can seed a division-healing kind of love!

Healing/Reconciling Action: Be even more active in your learning about the other person or group by making notes about things you would like to remember that you did not previously understand about their circumstances. Reach out in some concrete way to the person or group you have identified. Learn about advantages you may have had that others were blocked from. Let your respect show you are open to listen and learn. My big sister used to ask me: "Why do you have two ears and only one tongue?" The answer: So we can listen twice as much as we speak!

8

SHARED MEANING
Love's Choreographer

"Meaning arises not in either subject or object, but in the shared wisdom...that arises in the "between..."
~ Pamela Cooper-White, *Shared Wisdom* ~

People seek meaning in their lives. Seeking and making meaning are universal human endeavors that are closely connected with the ability to make loving connections with other people.

"May I have this dance?"

The boarding school I attended was all-male. Our exclusively male world made us ambivalent about the twice-yearly dances arranged with the girl boarders from the convent across town. We were excited but also nervous. A good bit of time was spent clinging to the walls, being "wallflowers," I think it used to be called. We tried to look nonchalant but, in fact, we were worried we might be rejected or in some way make a fool of ourselves if we asked for a dance.

Love is a bit like that. We hold back because we may not have the right "moves." We easily miss out on love's growing place — that rich but messy place between lovers where meaning begins to be shared and love becomes a possibility.

Meaning-making between lovers starts small and is often clumsy.

"Is he going to ask me to dance or not?!"

"He keeps looking over here. Shy, I suppose. But if only he knew. I'm kinda like that too. Feeling pretty scared myself."

"Only four girls left who aren't dancing. Hope I'm not the last."

"She seems quiet. May be my type. But I wonder if she's a good dancer. I'm sure to step on her feet and that won't go over well."

To flourish, love first needs connection, no matter how untidy and clumsy that connection may be. Love's growth needs mutual responsiveness and accountability between partners or groups. In that shared "dance," meaning evolves — which contributes to the depth and viability of the relationship. As the "dance" continues, shared meaning suggests new steps. Shared meaning choreographs new moves.

We are on a quest for a special kind of love, a robust kind of love that we have named Justice-Love. Its aim is to bring healing and reconciliation. In the quest for Justice-Love, shared meaning between individuals or groups is essential but not easy to come by. When things are going well, people hardly notice that they are seeking and making meaning in their lives.

But when severe setbacks occur, both the need for meaning and the challenge of finding it become apparent. Life's tragedies inhibit the search for meaning while at the same time crying out for it. Parents lose a child. Gentrification in a neighborhood puts home ownership out of reach for the original residents. Grief and desperate questioning follow. Why? Why? Why? What's the point of it all? Why us? Why me?

Even after the storm of rage and grief has calmed, shared meaning continues to be a big challenge. "I know there's really no good side to losing Holly. But maybe we can make our love and time together an even greater priority now. I love you so much," offers one spouse.

"I just can't go there. This has been a nightmare for me," responds the other. "You know how precarious my work situation has been. This is just the last thing I needed to happen right now. You know I'm not even sure what you think a shrink is going to do. No disrespect intended."

The greatest human tragedies are those which drive people, groups, even whole countries apart. Their anger breeds hostility and violence. Their distancing from each other brings "othering" in the worst sense of that word—putting down and assuming the worst of the "other" person or group. Justice-love seems to have its work cut out for it!

"So let's get started. Welcome everyone. Just meeting the way we are today seems like a cause for celebration. The first steps toward understanding and reconciliation."

"Excuse me. Isn't it a bit early for the word reconciliation? Many of us were reluctant to come to this meeting. What are we "reconciling?" Do you even have a clue what we have been going through?"

But the drive to find meaning keeps trying to break through. And when it does, the possibility of *shared* meaning can bring hope for reconciliation. In his book *Man's Search for Meaning* (2006), Viktor Frankl described this remarkable phenomenon. Writing about survival in Nazi death camps, he said: "Those who have a 'why' to live can bear with almost any 'how.'" One might change that slightly and say: "Those who have a 'why' to 'love' can bear the struggle of getting there."

Meaning-making and meaning-sharing are critical steps on the way to reconciliation and healing. Their importance brings us back to the need for self-reflection and other-reflection. The "dance" of love has been interrupted. If the "dance" of love is to start moving again toward reconciliation and healing, a safe space needs to be created where alienated people can begin to discover shared meaning. The humility of honest self-reflection contributes to that safety. The respectful listening and learning of other-reflection increases it.

Opening ourselves to new meanings and understandings can be transformative. I don't enjoy Hip-hop music. I began to suspect that my dislike of it went hand in hand with a lot of my own prejudices. I enrolled for a seminar about Hip-hop and learned a huge amount— not only about Hip-hop but also about my own negative assumptions. The best part of all was that starting immediately at the seminar itself, I benefited from a new area of shared meaning to replace the false assumptions that had arisen in my isolation.

I received a phone call from Abram, a student I had taught many years before and not heard from since. He would be connecting flights at JFK. Would I be interested in meeting there for a couple of hours? You bet I would!

The reunion was wonderful. As we said goodbye and he prepared to board his flight, he turned back to me. "I have never forgotten your classes. You kept our hope alive. Thank you!"

The students in those classes loved getting me side-tracked off the required Catholic syllabus. We would talk about the suffering and hopelessness experienced by their families at home. We would talk about the bravery of their parents teetering on the brink of despair and yet clinging to hope and providing for their children's care. We would talk about their own bravery in refusing to give up. All those many years later, Abram was saying that was exactly what they needed to talk about. Those deviations from a class focused on dry dogma made room for meaning-making and meaning-sharing. They made the future paths of those students much more than hopeless and dangerous ones. Academic knowledge stepped aside to make room for the meaning which brings hope.

Relationships are opportunities for shared meaning and mutual healing. Surprising relationship treasures often pop up in the shared space between people or groups who are trying to understand each other. The back and forth of a relationship is a rich opportunity for mutual learnings, shared meaning, respect, and appropriately-boundaried affection. Shared meaning is best discovered in an "I-Thou" relationship between mutually honoring co-subjects rather than an "I-It" relationship based on hierarchy and power which often treats others as objects.

Shared meaning is an important milestone on the journey to Justice-Love.

Self-Reflection: What gives purpose and passion to your life and work? Do you have a sense of why it may have lost its power? How might you refocus on the meaning that most energizes your loving outreach to others? As you contemplate the importance of shared meaning with those you wish to love, ask yourself what attitudes and assumptions of yours could be blocking it.

Other-Reflection: Think of the other person (or each person in a group) as "Thou," a wonderful human being worthy of your utmost respect.

Are you trapped in your assumptions about what should bring meaning to others? Assumptions which block you from deeper listening and learning? Can you roll back your assumptions? Can you ask (if appropriate) or at least research what might be important to others in their meaning-making? Will you examine their very own meaning-making in contrast to your assumptions about it!

Healing/Reconciling Action: Start with a particular person/group that you tend to make assumptions about. Put your assumptions on pause. Research in whatever respectful way you are able, some aspects of that person or group you have probably overlooked. In the case of a group, you might start by reading a book that sheds new light for you on the history and experience of that group. In the case of an individual, proceed cautiously if trust is not yet such that you can ask many questions. (In that case your initial action will be to work on the mutual respect that will build trust!) Have you ever thought of signing up for an anti-racism training to perhaps learn something you haven't considered before? Not because your employer requires it, but simply because you want to learn and open yourself to reconciling love?

9

THE REAL YOU
Love Needs a Healthy Self

"We all have an infant inside of us, but the
infant doesn't have to run the show!"
~ Murray Bowen ~

It's hard to give or receive love if you are not reasonably confident in yourself and willing to keep growing into the real you. If you don't feel OK about who you are, attempts to love often falter and become less about the other person and more about your needs. I'm sure you have heard someone in frustration say about their partner that they sometimes feel as if they have an extra child. It's a hard saying, of course, but very often contains a grain of truth. Love is a work in progress! There's always room for it to grow. And love's growth is linked to our own ongoing growth. The firming up of a healthy self is an important part of generating healing love. We need to keep growing so that love can keep growing!

In his family systems theory, Murray Bowen highlights a common obstacle to growing a robust and healthy independent self: difficulty separating in a healthy manner from one's original family. (*See murraybowenarchives.org.*) Sometimes it is hard for people to separate their own "grown-up" emotional functioning from the way emotions functioned in their original families. It is hard for them to "self-differentiate." They can get stuck in the powerful processes that were, and may still be, operating in their original families. Their own growth suffers, and so does their ability to love.

I met Bowen once at a conference he was leading. When I told him who I was, he said: "Really? Is that who you *really* are?" He was teasing me because "authentic self" was the theme of the whole conference. But his lighthearted challenge rang true and was unforgettable. It was a small moment of "continuing education" that would continue to require self-examination throughout my professional career and my family life.

As a young priest quietly going about my business in a traditional priestly role, I was unexpectedly thrust into an activist role. It brought out in me a lot of fear and exposed the work I needed to do on self-differentiation. I worked in an area that had been chosen by the apartheid government for one of its infamous "resettlement" schemes. People were dumped in the arid veld with scant resources under the blatantly false pretext that they were being "resettled" in their true "homeland." A priest friend had been doing courageous work supporting the people and exposing the government's nefarious schemes and the police served him with deportation papers. He had to leave for his home country of Holland within three days or risk being detained. At his urgent request—and with trepidation—I took over his work the very next day. As a South African citizen, I did not risk deportation, but I knew from personal experience that the police intimidation he had suffered would now be visited upon me in some form or another.

But it was not the police I truly feared. Both my family and religious superiors were against the apartheid government—but in a "respectable" conformist kind of way. I had a lot of that "respectable conformism" in me. How would my family and my superiors feel about my taking on a more activist role?

Predictably, both my family and immediate religious superiors were "concerned." They encouraged me to get back to what they considered my "proper" priestly work as soon as possible.

But it didn't stop me from embracing the call to work for justice. In fact, this was a critical point in my life. "Growth" had called and somehow I had managed to answer the call. My life was set on a new trajectory that made possible further growth in the future. My acceptance of the call had brought me up against the "self" that

42

sat comfortably preparing my next sermon while injustice raged all around me! The need for self-differentiation challenged the comfortable "self," whose fearful reaction grew directly out of an obedient, conforming upbringing. It challenged that "self" to stretch beyond the comfort of attachment to family and become its own "self" that confidently ruled its own actions. Accepting such a challenge, even with trepidation, can help Justice-Love grow and further the cause of justice. It was certainly a turning point for me, and my report on the government's reprehensible actions was read in parliament by its sole Progressive member, the courageous Helen Suzman. An additional resource to help her keep resistance and hope alive in a very difficult time (Suzman, 1993, p. 80).

Those lingering concerns about how the family would feel and my fear of disappointing them would come up again at other significant times in my life. It became critically important that I learn to distinguish between any perceived external pressures the family was putting on me (often none whatsoever in reality), and the much more significant internal pressures I was continuing to put on myself.

I was raised in a staunchly Roman Catholic family in which three of the five children embraced religious vocations. Eight years of my schooling were in a strict Roman Catholic boarding school. For many reasons, I began to feel the church was no longer a community in which I could grow, thrive, and be a happy and fulfilled human being.

But whenever I thought about leaving the Roman Catholic church, a picture would form in my mind of my staunchly Catholic father and how disappointed he would be. Then, after he died, a picture would form in my mind of my staunchly Catholic big sister and how disappointed *she* would be! At last, I became aware that my particular stuckness was not a matter of religious conviction but a matter of "family loyalty." But not the healthy kind of loyalty. It wasn't a struggle about belief but of differentiating myself from my original family. I continue to honor and respect the sincere commitment to the Catholic faith of my parents, my siblings and their families. But that is not the same as feeling constrained to do likewise. Many are able to relate to the difficulties of leaving the nest in a healthy way. Because it's a matter of ongoing growth, some of us have to "leave the nest" several times during our lives!

On occasion, a person's lack of self-differentiation exhibits not in fear of leaving the family but in a brash projection of over-entitlement and loud (but suspect) overconfidence. The healthy self we seek is not at all the same as the puffed up self-important "self" often popularly referred to as "ego." Love needs a healthy self—not an overblown blustery "ego." The overblown ego is often a dead giveaway that healthy self-differentiation has been feared and avoided.

Sometimes people try to escape from the hard work of healthy self-differentiation by simply cutting off contact with parents or other family members. That may give a temporary "sense" of relief—but wherever we go we tend to carry with us the consequences of an inadequate differentiation from family. We may move away or cut ourselves off and think we've "solved" the problem—that they are no longer influencing our lives in a problematic way. But then our lack of differentiation is likely to rear its ugly head in other ways. Without realizing it we may find our "stuckness" cropping up in other relationships, and inevitably affecting our ability to give and receive love.

Lack of a healthy differentiation from family can show itself in many different ways. Maybe you have recognized that some of your blocks to reaching out in love are related to self-differentiation. Resolve to reflect about this and get help if it seems to be needed. No need to be self-critical—healthy self-differentiation is a lifelong project for most of us. But it is of great value for any person seeking to grow in Justice-Love.

Self-Reflection: Some quiet daily reflection can go a long way to motivating work on self-differentiation. Under what social or relationship circumstances do you find yourself either overreacting, or stuck and unable to react at all? Overwhelmed by fear and unable to react in a constructive way? A situation in which fear or other emotions seem to get the better of you? You may be stuck in the powerful emotional system that operated in your original family. It may have served some purpose long ago but is no longer helpful in your current situation. Progress you make in freeing yourself will help you grow a calm non-reactive self. You will be much better equipped to reach out to others with a reconciling love.

Other-Reflection: Think of the other person (or each person in a group) as "Thou," a wonderful human being worthy of your utmost respect.

When you think about difficulties you have that may come from your parents or original family, do you automatically feel angry and blaming? Even if your insight is correct, could you try a more open reflection about those relationships? This is important because blame by itself will often add to your own paralysis about any change. Try to imagine what it might have been like for your parents to deal with whatever they were dealing with in their original family. What original-family issues may others you aspire to love be dealing with?

Healing/Reconciling Action: If continuing to work on your own self-differentiation seems to be a critical issue for you, consider what steps you might take. Does working on this directly with family members seem doable? Is it a frightening prospect? Consider working with a therapist to help with this. You may need support in taking some helpful actions. Better to get the support than to let years go by without doing anything about it. And certainly if this seems to be a critical issue for you, set aside lots more time for reflection about it. Remember that truth is revealed best through quiet reflection. Truth is powerful. It can propel you towards your next steps in growth and ultimately to your next loving action! You may be ready right now to take the courageous step of reaching out to a person from whom you have become estranged. Find a way to take a first respectful step.

10

THE GROUNDED HEALER
Love's "Earthy" Roots

*"To be rooted is perhaps the most important and
least recognized need of the human soul"*
~ Simone Weil ~

We've talked about the importance for Justice-Love of being present in the moment. Being truly "there" (not somewhere else) is equally important. Being truly present to each encounter whether with our inner self, another person or a task. It's called being "grounded" — the ability to live our lives and conduct our relationships out of a deep and stable place. Being grounded applies both physically and mentally — being physically able to pause our tendency to be constantly on the move, and mentally able to calm our minds from wandering away from the task at hand or, more importantly, from a precious human encounter.

Many cartoons these days show people glued to their cell phones in restaurants or around kitchen tables — where one might expect a special effort to connect with each other. Lightheartedly, they illustrate how easily we use technology to take us away from where we are. But when we are finished chuckling, we should be concerned about how this encourages us to flit from one distraction to another and favors superficial encounters over deeper connection. We have become accustomed to living and relating without being grounded.

This ungroundedness is especially concerning when the disconnection blocks the cultivation of Justice-Love. If our lives are a constant distraction from getting to know ourselves deep within, our ability to relate to others is also impaired. It's even worse if our superficial and ungrounded living makes us quickly look elsewhere for answers.

Less than 30 years after the courageous pastor Dietrich Bonhoeffer was hanged for standing up to Hitler, a few of us sat in a room in Durban, South Africa with Bonhoeffer's best friend and biographer Eberhard Bethge. He and his wife Renate (Bonhoeffer's niece) had graciously agreed to be with us as we struggled to confront the worsening oppression of apartheid. We needed all the guidance and encouragement we could get.

The very presence of the Bethges was an encouragement and an inspiration, of course, and they gave us many insights. But I hoped for specific answers. I sat there with bated breath, notebook in hand. What would Eberhard and Renate advise?

You know what they said? "We come to you with love and in solidarity. We do not bring answers for your context. You have those answers inside yourselves and you also have those answers in the love and sharing between yourselves."

I thought, *What!!?? No answers?! We brought you all the way from Europe!*

But in fact, it wasn't a let-down at all. On the contrary, it was an amazing lightning bolt of awareness about our own responsibility and inner resources. It was empowering! Nobody else was going to do this for us. The answers were inside us and we needed to go deep. We had the answers and we needed to listen to each other — especially to the most vulnerable and marginalized among us.

Resources and answers we seek are nearer than we think — if we pause and look inward. They are often right under our noses and in the midst of our own struggling communities.

Ambition and the drive for "success" are often the culprits in getting us ungrounded. The drive for success can be like a horse running wild. The horse demands so much attention and energy to keep it on the trail that our journeys and destinations are thrown into confusion. We can become distracted from our original goals and see our initial passions depleted, exhausting ourselves in the process.

But the biggest problem with untamed ambition is that it disconnects us from our original "grounding," our necessary rootedness in the wholesome life-giving earth. It disconnects us from the humble earth from which we have come and to which we will return. *Humus* is the Latin word for "earth" and the root of the English word "humility." Humility, healthy groundedness, knowing our appropriate place in the Universe grows out of what we do with the messiness, the "earthiness" of life. And that includes the messes we ourselves so often make.

Sometimes, however, our messes make us feel shame and humiliation—which are not at all the same as humility! The word humiliation (also from the Latin root *humus*) describes a very different reality—a reality that puts us at risk for being sucked down into the mud for a useless wallowing session.

But the "mud" of humiliation is also an opportunity to learn and grow. We can change humiliation into the virtue of humility. Thich Nhat Hanh writes that the Buddha said, "You cannot grow lotus on marble. You have to grow it in mud!" (2004). Humility is calming and grounding. Perhaps more than anything else, it equips us for our journey toward Justice-Love.

Another thing that can unground us is a bit too much need for affirmation and praise. For its growth, an infant quite appropriately needs to be admired, so parents and others "coo" and smile. We continue to need a bit of this treatment throughout our lives though we have a hard time admitting it. You could call it "normal" narcissism. We all need some affirmation and encouragement. As the baby needs a dose of it appropriate to its stage of development, so do we need a dose of it appropriate to *our* stage.

But if we need a degree of affirmation that is inconsistent with a more mature stage of growth, it is problematic. Too much hunger for attention and affirmation from outside ourselves can dislodge our healthy roots in the good earth. It can stop us from being present where we are and should be. And cause us to go searching all over the place for something that is close at hand—as close as our calm self-reflection about our place in the Universe. The late poet John O'Donohue puts it well: "The greatest pilgrimage is the one that brings us home to ourselves" (O'Donohue, 1999).

I facilitated a seminar once and made the mistake of glancing at the evaluations before starting on the two-hour drive home. At a quick glance, the evaluations looked overwhelmingly positive. Apparently, that wasn't good enough for me — one person felt quite negative about my presentation. Instead of being buoyed by the positive responses, I spent the journey home obsessing about — even angry about — the single negative one. My narcissism, not so far below the surface, had found an opportunity to come up for breath! He's needy. He's tired. Let's get him now!!

Maybe on a better day, a day when I was feeling calmer and better about myself, I would have had less of a need to be loved and affirmed by every single one of the seminar attendees. As it was, I was almost home before I was able to calm down and laugh about my need for so much affirmation.

If things like ambition and obsessing about future "success" can disconnect us from our roots, what can we do about it?

The closest bus stop to my childhood home still left us a long steep climb to the front door. On the way up, I would huff and puff and complain. My sister, older and wiser, told me to stop looking up the hill toward the house and rather look down at my feet. The climb immediately became more pleasant and went more quickly!

I have found that "under your nose" therapy and "under your nose" reflection are by far the best antidotes when our hunger for success or affirmation lures us away from being grounded in the earth of humility. People are often surprised when I ask them, "What is supposed to be under your nose right now?" But they soon realize that our attention and enthusiasm is best spent on what we are supposed to be doing right now. In other words, we must attend to what's "under our noses" — the priorities of our current jobs, vocations, relationships. Those things are what, if done to the best of our ability, most likely will contribute to our future success.

There's no harm in having dreams about future aspirations but only if they are appropriately contained so as not to contaminate or deplete the present "under your nose" undertaking. Useless focus on the future, being held captive in the future, stealing committed present time to work on future dreams frequently result in little satisfaction and a lot of tension. This ungroundedness frequently and tragically leads away from instead of toward the Justice-Love our world so desperately needs.

The number of ungrounded people in influential positions is quite alarming. Advancement has become more dependent on a desire for money and less on proven competence. Self-serving politicians flagrantly bend their beliefs and principles (or pretend to) so that they can get the support they need to attain high office. We end up with "leaders" who really haven't excelled at the duties that were "right under their noses" — people who are ungrounded from their personal growth and civic duty and focused instead on "success" and a prized position for which they are quite often unsuited.

Instead, we need grounded leaders who are capable of self-reflection and sincere other-reflection to carry them and lead all of us toward Justice-Love.

———————

Self-Reflection: Do your aspirations and ambitions for the future move you away from anchoring yourself in the present in a healthy way? As a result do you notice yourself neglecting what deserves your focus and attention right here right now? Do you neglect the things that are right under your nose, that if you attended to in a mindful present way, might help you be less anxious? Might actually help you attain your future goals without your constant plotting and planning? Could you put aside a day of personal reflection on which you do an inventory of the things that make it hard for you to be grounded?

Other-Reflection: Think of the other person (or each person in a group) as "Thou," a wonderful human being worthy of your utmost respect.

Sometimes people's lives are so demanding, so focused on survival for self and dependents, that it is hard for them to be calm and present. Try to see every person's life in a broader context so that you can get a better picture of what causes them pain and anxiety. Put yourself in their shoes — in the moment.

Healing/Reconciling Action: Rework your daily schedule and priorities, giving the appropriate amount of quality time to the worthwhile pursuits you have already signed up for. Focus on your current work obligations and your current personal mission statement as you engage in this revised planning and prioritizing. Without abandoning your dreams for the future, keep them compartmentalized and in check so that they don't take you away from what is "right under your nose" today! Consider a hobby that focuses on the process and enjoyment of the activity rather than the result, e.g., learning to paint as opposed to producing a masterpiece. Best of all, the work to be done right under your nose may have to do with healing relationships or working for justice in your community.

11

DO YOU HEAR ME NOW?
Static on the Love Channel

"Attention is the rarest and purest form of generosity"
~ Simone Weil ~

Respectful attention, deep listening, and learning are critically important skills for the person who aspires to bring reconciliation and healing to relationships. Our self- and other-reflections at the end of each chapter have been helping us develop these skills.

Defensiveness and defensive anger are huge blocks to reconciliation work. People feel attacked and put down when a would-be reconciler, no matter how well-intentioned, assumes she understands the situation and feelings of the other person or group.

To get beyond argument and defense or assumptions and denials, self-reflection and other-reflection are extremely important. They set the tone for a humble, non-invasive, non-"know it all" approach. Such an approach makes it less likely that the other person will feel the need to defend by closing off or attacking.

Better still if we can assume the spirit of Simone Weil and offer the "purest form of generosity" — attention.

Many years as a relationship therapist helped me see just how rare that kind of generous attention is. And without it a lot of "static" occurs on the "Love Channel." We often don't really hear each other — and our partners may eventually switch it off all together. Generous, caring attention, on the other hand, clears up the static and makes us more inclined to listen and respond.

Let's look more closely at that kind of generous attention.

To become more attentive, we need to get in touch with our own feelings, needs and motivations. Unless we have a good sense of what is going on in us, we are unlikely to understand what could be pulling us away from the attention we would like to give to a person we want to love.

As each of our four children went through the challenges of their teenage years, I temporarily stopped accepting adolescent referrals to my practice. Distractions from dealing with our own family's teen issues would sometimes cling to me as I returned to the counseling office. Occasionally, I was on the verge of allowing these issues and my feelings about them to influence how I would conduct the treatment of a teen client. Learnings in one's own family can be quite useful, but not if they are applied to situations where they don't belong.

Our generous attention is critically important when our goal is to heal a vulnerable person or bring reconciliation to a situation of injustice. An important aspect of paying loving attention is to know when our own "stuff" is getting in the way of healing love.

Clients often attach to healers feelings that really belong to other relationships or situations. So there are a lot of feelings going back and forth. But it is the healer's responsibility to tune the Love Channel and get rid of as much static as possible. One of the strategies I used to remain attentive in spite of any negative reaction I might experience to a client's anger was to project a large imaginary "empathy screen" on the wall behind the person. On it was a list of all the difficult relationship issues, losses, and trauma this wonderful human being had experienced that would bring him to the current negative feelings that he was sending in my direction.

In one case, this trick was especially important to my being able to hold onto healing love. My negative feelings toward an older teen began in the waiting room and were already getting worse as we walked down the hall to my office. He was dressed "goth" style all in black and with lethal looking chains dangling. His anger at having to come to see me was palpable.

How was I to love him when my own negative reactions were already snapping into place? In the context of my upbringing, especially boarding school, this was a person who simply needed to be "whipped back into shape" both figuratively and literally.

My "empathy screen" got me through the first two or three sessions. "Father died when he was seven. Two angry and emotionally absent stepfathers have since come and gone in his life. Mother can't cope and alternates between smothering and screaming him away."

I was potentially just another one of those disappointing adults in his life. Though my attention may not have been terribly "generous" to begin with, I was able to hang on for dear life and the therapy became a positive experience for him — and for me.

Ongoing reflection about what's going on in one's self and what's going on in the "other" are very important when there's static on the Love Channel. Honest self-reflection and caring other-reflection produce a static-free atmosphere in which people can begin to really hear each other and find common ground.

Without genuine, generous attention to another in pain, Justice-Love is unattainable.

Self-reflection: We would be the rarest of people if we did not sometimes have quite negative reactions toward other people. Such negative feelings and reactions are especially significant if they occur with persons who are close to us, important in our community, or among persons or groups with whom we aspire to a better relationship. Are you able to open yourself to take a good hard look at your reactions and reflect on any part of those reactions that have more to do with you and your needs, past experiences, prejudices, than they do with the person you are reacting to?

Other-Reflection: Think of the other person (or each person in a group) as "Thou," a wonderful human being worthy of your utmost respect.

Ponder the attributes in another person that bring out your anger or fear or judgment. Allow that the attributes you think you are perceiving, may be based in pain or difficulty of which you are not aware — pain or difficulty or a background story that you might greatly benefit from trying to learn and understand.

Healing/Reconciling Action: Holding onto this more open and non-judgmental attitude, try anew to reach out to a person with whom you formerly felt blocked. Be courageous and patient. Taking responsibility for your own blocks to love and taking steps to remove those blocks is usually noticed by the other person. Soon they may be willing to do the same.

12

HEALING FOR ALL
Love's Wide Embrace

"Diversity is being invited to the party;
inclusion is being asked to dance."
~ Verna Myers ~

Justice-Love has a wide embrace — of all of humanity, no exceptions. People make mistakes, fall on hard times, take advantage of "the system," act unjustly, behave immorally, and sometimes commit crimes. But that does not mean they forfeit the right to be treated in a humane and just manner or to be given help in pursuing the basics needed for safety, well-being and human dignity. Justice-Love is not meted out by judges and juries, politicians, religious leaders or by anyone's judgment about who deserves and who does not deserve. Justice-Love is deeper than all these and derives its authority and agency from the fact that we are bound together in our common humanity.

We must be ready to offer that kind of wide embrace. We must be alert to whatever threatens to block inclusion into the embrace of Justice-Love.

We can easily deceive ourselves into thinking inclusiveness is "going quite well, thank you" in our society. It's heartening to see so many institutions signing on to the need for "Diversity, Equity and Inclusion (DEI)" initiatives.

Programs are set up, trainings given — but there is a great deal of resistance to them in many companies. People attend with reluctance. Some say they are a waste of time, that "political correctness" is at the center, or that enough is already being done.

Those who aspire to spread Justice-Love would do well to dig deeply into the concepts of diversity, equity and inclusion so they are not easily swayed by the suggestion that we have "done enough."

Studies abound which show how access to housing, health care, maternal health services, employment, loans, financial assistance, voting, and many other services is limited and sometimes blocked completely because of injustices — embedded in the delivery system itself or in the prejudiced attitudes of those responsible for providing the services.

Access is also blocked when providers lack the understanding and sensitivity needed to deliver services in a just manner. Strict job requirements, lack of transportation, confusing insurance regulations, disadvantage many people before they have even arrived at the waiting room. Just and effective provision of services also requires cultural competence. Providers of services must understand the specific needs, fears and language barriers of people from cultures different from their own. Systemic racism, homophobia and a whole slate of other "isms" cause flawed outcomes that result in injustice. To be a loving healer demands an understanding of this and a commitment to training and ongoing supervision.

Justice-Love work is demanding work. There are challenges along the way. Sometimes those challenges are systemic, due to deeply entrenched and often unrecognized injustices built into society's institutions over years. As a result, those challenges are often multiplied through understandable resistance and fear in chronically oppressed people. Why should they trust anyone claiming to work for justice and reconciliation?

They may be put off by a person's approach. They find it intolerable when someone who knows hardly anything about them assumes to know what is best for them.

Feelings run high and relationships between people or groups deteriorate rapidly. Well-intended relationships become hurtful. People say things they regret. Emotions cause people to push each other away.

None of this means love is doomed. It only means that a hurting person may need a wider place in which to "bounce around," — a place where they can feel confident that disapproval does not mean abandonment. A place where they can sense that the "wide embrace" is still firmly in place and they can rely on it. A place where a person seeking to heal shows humility rather than all-knowing arrogance, genuine love rather than patronizing assumptions.

Justice-Love must be ready to extend that kind of wide embrace because unjust situations are messy and off-putting. They can take time to remedy. Our passion for justice waxes and wanes. Something inspires us and we have great plans, and then time passes by and we find too often that we have done very little.

Understanding the importance and value of the "wide embrace" can give us a wider view and courage to take action. If the going gets tough, the wide embrace can help us persevere.

If you care about Justice-Love, you may be branded by conspiracy theorists as weak. They may portray you as unable to keep people safe from crime or to keep immigrants from taking their jobs. You may be called a "socialist," in an attempt to brand your views as dangerous and misguided.

In the face of this, as you move toward Justice-Love, it is that much more important not to reflexively become argumentative and defensive. Quiet study and reflection become all the more important. Only loving listening produces an atmosphere in which a constructive conversation can eventually take place.

Do not confuse this with passivity — or giving up. Although chaos and misinformation caused by conspiracy theories are extremely discouraging — and many throw up their hands in despair of ever being able to stop their effects — the wide embrace of Justice-Love requires us to persevere. We must keep on educating ourselves and others — protecting young people from disinformation, holding people and institutions accountable, and being prominent leaders in promoting truth and objective sources of truth.

Even things considered "progressive" can be blocks to justice when only a privileged section of the population, with more money or access, benefits. "Progress" is not based in Justice-Love if it is unaffordable or inaccessible to people, especially those who desperately need the services.

My work across many cultures and different sociological strata has made me suspicious of "new" approaches to healing that take many books to explain, many hours to implement, or an obscene amount of money, especially from a person needing help. Justice-Love is transferable across oceans, cultures, and socioeconomic strata.

Accessibility to all is key. If you claim some tremendous merit or potency for your special approach or technique, then show its applicability, effectiveness, and affordability across a wide range of people. If your approach cannot be simplified and streamlined for use with the common person, then it needs to be named for what it likely is—a rare medicine for the few rather than a proven help for the many.

Unfortunately, this is not the way it usually works. Look at the hundreds of ads on social media, proclaiming a revolutionary cure for something. A first book may indeed offer a few useful, though limited, resources but is too quickly followed by another. Soon the new approach is being advertised as indispensable for the healer, requiring "responsible" healers to invest in the necessary training and become "certified."

I practiced for more than 30 years as a dually-licensed Marriage and Family Therapist and Clinical Social Worker. I was meticulous about observing the continuing education requirements of both licenses. I was honored when colleagues affirmed my work and often referred "difficult" cases to me, or sought my consultation or clinical supervision of challenging situations within their own practice.

I have been quite open to new learning and have attended many seminars about this or that new approach or technique. But here's the telling thing. In a few cases, the approaches proved effective and it was great to have them in my toolkit. But for the vast majority of the situations I dealt with over the years, only a few basic "tried and true" principles brought the best results.

For 30 years, two beautiful seashells sat on the coffee table right in front of my clients. One shell was smooth and shiny with beautiful camouflage markings that had originally made it impossible to see when against the backdrop of all the other vibrant marine life. Clearly an example of defense by hiding or by almost disappearing. The other shell was frightening in its spikiness and jaggedness. "I won't hide," it seemed to shout, "but don't you dare come near me!"

I genuinely believe that conversations about these two shells helped my clients more than any book or system of therapy to think about their own way of being in the world, and whether it helped them heal.

There is no doubt that technical know-how is often important for healing. But those who aspire to be loving healers must be humble learners of another person's sacred terrain—not technicians following a procedure. Our effectiveness as healers and reconcilers comes not from an elitist initiation or a gold-framed license. Rather it is a function of our humble acceptance of an invitation to enter a person's sacred space.

In summary, the effective practice of healing love that is transferable across oceans, cultures and social strata is grounded in a universal ethic of love, equality and justice. Justice-Love's embrace is wide and inclusive.

Self-Reflection: Are you convinced that you know best how to love a person? If your thoughts have been heavily weighted toward a feeling that you know exactly what to do, can you think of occasions when that attitude may have resulted in your excluding someone or some group from the very healing love you intended to offer? When you review approaches you have used in an effort to relate more lovingly to others, are there some you now recognize as blocking rather than facilitating closeness?

In what circumstances, past or present, do you find yourself most discouraged or close to giving up? Have you felt "put down" for your sincere beliefs about justice and how to attain it? Can your feelings nudge you toward deeper empathy for those who are discouraged because they suffer injustice?

Other-Reflection: Think of the other person (or each person in a group) as "Thou," a wonderful human being worthy of your utmost respect.

Isabel Wilkerson (*Caste*, 2020) defines "radical empathy" as "putting in the work to educate oneself and to listen with a humble heart to understand another's experience from their perspective, not as we imagine we would feel." Focus on a person with whom you would like to build a more loving relationship. What listening and learning might you need to do? Does the concept of the wide embrace help you with this?

Healing/Reconciling Action: Dedicate some quality time to a particular person (perhaps go for a walk) and use the time to ask (non-intrusively) some questions you have never asked them before, questions that may lead you to get to know the person in a new way. If you have always assumed you know all there is to know about some group, now may be the time to study that group's history in more depth. If your relationship with a member of that group is such that it will be well-received, perhaps it is time to ask some respectful questions.

13

TRUTH TO POWER
Love Speaks the Truth

"Love is not a weak, spineless emotion; it is a
powerful moral force on the side of justice."
~ Bernice A. King ~

Sometimes on a busy day I used to treat myself to a Baskin-Robbins shake or some ice cream. I thought it better not to tell Jane because she would just worry about my health.

Then, we had friends over for dinner and decided to go to Baskin-Robbins afterwards for a special dessert. When the server got to me she said, "And you, sir? Your usual?"

Busted! Needless to say, I've never heard the end of it. If only concerns about honesty and transparency in our society were as inconsequential as a little guilty conscience about too much ice cream.

Unfortunately, truth and transparency are hard to find these days even in the crucially important matter of how we govern our society and make just decisions for the benefit of all. My concerns are often waved off by people admonishing me to "get real" and understand that deception has always been a part of politics and government.

No. Not this way, it hasn't!

If polls are even a little bit accurate, it's clear that a very large number of people agree with the politicians who say that truth and accountability don't matter. Only winning matters. Social platforms and other cyber resources that could be used to benefit our society are instead used to warp the truth and win peoples' allegiance based on dangerous lies. Outrageous conspiracy theories are propagated to manipulate people through fear. In the worst cases, hate and violence are stirred up. All this in a society crying out for more collaboration and cohesion.

I have been disappointed in the outcome of many elections in my lifetime—both abroad and in the US. And I have witnessed the understandable disappointment of many losing "sides."

But I have never seen more blatant and irresponsible refusals to be accountable to the truth than are evident now. Some are blatant in embracing lies. Others are complicit by their silence. Many refuse to speak up and counter harmful disinformation and dangerous fear-based messages they know to be untrue.

More than ever, we need courageous justice-seekers to stand up and be counted. We need people who are willing to work hard to seek the truth and then proclaim it. We might even call them "prophets."

I was first introduced to the concept of a "prophet" as primarily a person who "foretells the future." That definition has received so much attention that it obscures what is to me the truly consequential meaning—a person who sees things with the eyes of Truth and calls us to a world of justice for all people. A prophet of that ilk exposes self-serving dishonesty and proclaims truth, shakes people out of their selfish comfort and calls for change. A prophet calls out religious behavior that focuses too much on ritual and not enough on justice.

Justice-Love heeds that prophetic call. If love is to be more than sentimentality and self-gratification, then honesty, accountability and justice must be built into its very foundation. Imagine the healing potential if each partner in a relationship and each member of a group took it for granted that part of loving communication is "prophetic" communication. What if partners saw it as completely to be expected that love will sometimes compel them to speak hard uncomfortable truths to each other? What if they understood that painful honesty can help a relationship mature and thrive? What if they understood that even when it is best that a relationship end, sometimes painful honesty can ensure that the outcome is just toward all those affected, especially the more vulnerable.

In larger groups we can think of "love" as healthy cohesiveness or peaceful coexistence. If a community is to have those qualities in any lasting fashion, then honesty and accountability are essential ingredients. When they are lacking, "prophets" of honesty and accountability need to rise up. Truth needs to be spoken. Accountability needs to be demanded.

But prophets first need to HAVE the truth before they can proclaim it. Their truth and prophet credentials are suspect if they are not willing to do what it takes. And what it takes is humble and courageous research. Research that focuses not on making them look good but on shining a light on the truth. Claims of truth will always provoke accusations of subjectivity — but when prophets have done their research with sincerity and honesty, they need not fear such accusations. Prophetic seekers of Justice-Love must always be guided and anchored by their commitment to look deeply into themselves and into the situations of others. That is the most reliable research of all.

There are many things that lure people away from the truth and then lead to injustice. Perhaps none is as dangerous as false patriotism. While it is commendable to be loyal to one's country, that loyalty cannot be at the expense of the truth. Just as a couple should care for and cherish their relationship through honesty and mutual accountability, so also should the members of a country. Patriotism is never about "us" versus "them." It is not a weapon for "us" to use against "them." Patriotism celebrates the "we" and welcomes truth-seeking and mutual collaboration that promotes the wellbeing of all.

Nor is patriotism afraid of history. It does not apply a thick cosmetic paste to cover wrongdoings of the past. Not to acknowledge the ugly wounds of the past means present healing cannot take place. If the wounds inflicted by "ugly history" go unaddressed, they bleed still.

And no country is innocent of ugly history. In the US, peace, healthy cohesion, healthy thriving for all cannot come to pass until, for example, the fact that enslaved people were denied their rights as human beings for hundreds of years and that the lands and livelihoods of indigenous people were violently stolen are acknowledged.

In fact, we could all learn a lot from the healthy way original Americans approach history. In her book, *Braiding Sweetgrass*, Robin Wall Kimmerer writes that "in many Indigenous ways of knowing, time is not a river, but a lake in which the past, the present, and the future exist." We must not suppress the ugliness of the past and pretend it has conveniently flowed away. It has not.

Speaking truth to power, however, is not a call to arms or an attempt to monger fear. Stirring up fear is nearly always the first step in a process aimed at producing polarization. Instead, truth-seeking "prophets" cry out, "Rise up!" inviting all to honesty and mutual accountability, to a love for our wonderful country that is both appropriately self-interested but committed to the wellbeing of every person. It's not "My way or the highway." It's my way *and* yours.

How can we get together on this? How can we join in love based on truth, on science, on a willingness to listen attentively when our partners, our neighbors, and those most vulnerable to being hurt protest about unfairness?

By practicing Justice-Love, which speaks truth to power.

<hr />

Self-Reflection: What does "self-interest" mean to you? People say we are entitled to "vote our self-interest." Of course. I'm sure one way or another most of us do. But do your convictions about fairness include an ethic of fairness toward your neighbor, especially those neighbors who are most vulnerable to being hurt by a system that often favors one group over another? To what extent are you willing to speak the truth to powerful people, to dismantle systems that hurt your fellow human beings? Do your needs, prejudices, blindspots prevent you from seeing your own truth? Has this sometimes diminished your ability to be a "prophet" of truth?

Other-Reflection: Think of the other person (or each person in a group) as "Thou," a wonderful human being worthy of your utmost respect.

Are you sometimes too quick to proclaim your truth without putting in the work to "look deeply" into the circumstances and truth of another person or group? Has this stopped the process of reconciliation? Reflect on what you could do differently.

As you reflect on the person or group you aspire to love, ask yourself to what extent your love is still tinged with judgment about whether or not the person is deserving. Does this judgment make you lazy about pursuing their truth?

Healing/Reconciling Action: Prioritize a couple of situations in your life or community in which you feel a prophet is needed to speak truth to power. In what way could you be a part of such an intervention? What would you need to do to make sure you have the truth? How would you seek your community's help?

14

RECONCILIATION
Justice-Love's Reward

"There is no way to peace. Peace is the way."
~ A.J. Muste, Peace Activist ~

Justice-Love recognizes that forgiveness is an important part of its quest for reconciliation between people. But not "cheap" forgiveness.

Well intentioned religion, spirituality, and self-help often stress the need for the "wronged" person — unilaterally and magnanimously — to forgive. Too often when people encourage the practice of forgiveness, they are piously, though with good intention, referring to something cheap and easy — the turning of a switch in the mind, the change of an attitude, with little thought given to the need for a radical change in the underlying relationship. Little, if any, attention is given to the need for the hard work of reconciliation. I've heard people say, "It's for your own good. You don't want to be dominated and imprisoned by your inability to forgive!" or "It's what our religion or upbringing requires of us." When the sting of injustice makes a victim initially balk at a call to forgive, they are too many times made to feel they are wrong. But to forgive without requiring accountability is "cheap" forgiveness.

Sometimes forgiveness is cheapened by romantic stories that make it seem easy. And sometimes a kind of religious fervor soothes emotions in an escapist manner without committing to the hard work of reconciliation, reparation and healing. From a 1970s book and movie called "Love Story" emerged a famous but misleading quote: "Love means never having to say you're sorry!" In the ideal, this certainly describes a situation that can occur in trusting relationships.

Loving gestures and the return of a loving mood between people can sometimes take the place of the word "sorry."

But this should not be carelessly relied upon. It implies that "love" is a state of perfection in which people in relationship never hurt each other or the hurts are easily dealt with. Much more important is the need to recognize and explore the nature of another person's hurt, to be accountable, and to commit to whatever loving action can heal the wound...in time.

Prominent politicians and celebrities further cheapen the idea of forgiveness when they "walk back" statements made to offer an "apology" without accountability. "If anyone was offended by this...I offer my sincerest apologies!"

"If" implies that people really shouldn't have been offended, that there is no need for self- or other-reflection before or after on what was said. There is no accountability. No willingness to take responsibility for things said or actions taken.

Taking responsibility for an action that hurts another moves the matter into a sphere where true forgiveness is possible. If we forgive a person whose apology is empty, a person who refuses to be accountable for the part they play in the loss of trust, we exempt them from accountability and leave open the way to more injustice and exploitation instead of deep reconciliation. Victims of injustice must be careful not to let a spirit of goodwill or a tendency toward conflict avoidance blind them to the need to hold perpetrators accountable.

As a newly minted priest, I preached a "traditional" Christian sermon to apartheid-oppressed high-schoolers about the need to forgive and how suffering and patience would be rewarded in heaven. They shifted in their seats and their eyes glazed over. I blush to think of that sermon now, but it stimulated questions in their next class, like:

"How about we get a reward of some justice here and now on earth?"

"Are you saying we should simply accept our lot in life while these oppressors get off scot free?"

"Why should I passively accept injustice and forgive?"

"Doesn't that invite the person to hurt me more?"

"Why should I do the healing work and exempt him?"

These are healthy and understandable reactions from hurting people. (We've all asked these questions ourselves.) But in them are important lessons for all of us. Patience and forgiveness must be accompanied by accountability on the part of the person who has acted unjustly or been complicit in injustice — knowingly or otherwise.

Unless forgiveness emerges from the sincere, healthy and free inner work of the forgiver, there are many ways in which "forgiveness" can hinder instead of advance the process of reconciliation. "Easy" forgiveness, motivated by guilt, religious fervor or conflict avoidance, can both stunt the development of the forgiver and stop the potential for reconciliation in its tracks!

Forgiveness can be especially problematic if an injustice has been inflicted by persons or groups entrenched in and protected by structures of privilege and advantage. Wealth, privilege, and a comfortable "status quo" insulate people from any sense that they need forgiveness. If forgiveness is offered, they may even be indignant and self-righteous. Or they may feel entitled to be forgiven without taking any responsibility for injustice.

The old maxim "forgive and forget" is highly dangerous to a healthy and effective process of reconciliation. Attention to injustice from the past, which is far from ever being forgotten if no responsibility has been taken, must be an integral part of healing in the present.

Marital conflict is a simple example. In therapy sessions, I was often asked, "Why must she keep bringing up stuff from the past? Can't we just move forward?!" My usual answer was something like this: "I would certainly support you in that frustration if all she were doing was dredging stuff up to get back at you. But she seems to be saying she has never really experienced an acknowledgment from you of those past hurts and your responsibility for them. So those hurts are still right here with us in this room!"

There are, of course, challenges as we open ourselves to becoming reconcilers. There are some underlying dangers. The perpetrator of a wrong must be alert to the presence of a sense of entitlement to be forgiven, a tendency to diminish or gloss over the hurt that has been inflicted. Self-reflection and deep esteeming of the other person are critically important so that the expectation of forgiveness doesn't block the reconciliation process from getting off the ground.

Achieving the openness that comes from quiet self-reflection is not easy. In the rough and tumble of the world, we live in self-protective mode. We quickly jump to defensiveness. If we feel we are being blamed, we are quick to defend ourselves. If someone says our "privileged" status (or our immersion in a culture that gives us an unfair advantage over someone else) blinds us to the hurts being inflicted on other human beings, we are quick to deny it. "I am not responsible for what my ancestors did! I have pulled myself up by my bootstraps. Why can't they?"

If in a spirit of quiet humility, an atmosphere of self-honesty, we simply assume that there are ways in which we contribute to the hurts being experienced by our fellow human beings, there's no need for defensiveness. Just the responsibility to try and understand their points of view. Why should we be any different from everybody else? What would make us think we are so squeaky clean and blameless?

Forgiveness and reconciliation are often portrayed as the first steps on the journey of love. Why, then, are they at the very end of this little meditation manual? Because they aren't the first steps. Reconciliation is the END of a strenuous and often lengthy and complicated process.

The goal of our meditations has been to assist us in developing the self-honesty and humility necessary for us to take responsibility for the ways we may be complicit in unfairness to another person or group. Our meditations have been equipping us to engage in the process of developing Justice-Love. And we've learned that a lot of hard work and mutual accountability are involved so that we can repair something that was broken, and bring a state of reconciliation between individuals and groups.

Self-Reflection: What has your history been with forgiveness? Do you think of yourself as a forgiving person? Do you find it easy to forgive? Have you sometimes forgiven easily to avoid conflict? If you did that, do you think you let the other person off the hook? Any bad result for you? Do you need to be more careful about this in the future? What about expecting forgiveness from others? Have you sometimes felt impatient about it? Entitled to it? What do you think of the idea that healthy forgiveness can be a lengthy and demanding process? Perhaps your self-reflection can help you better understand how you can be most loving and effective in that process.

Other-Reflection: Think of the other person (or each person in a group) as "Thou," a wonderful human being worthy of your utmost respect.

Consider going back over the examples that have been given, noting especially the ones that had you struggling most with your defensiveness about needing to forgive. Even your annoyance that it is expected of you? Those are the instances where, if we keep up with the honest reflection, we are able to make the greatest contribution to healing!

Healing/Reconciling Action: Consider the history and hurts of a person or group that may be suspicious of or resistant to your efforts at reaching out to them in a forgiving way. How might they feel patronized or angry that you are making such an approach? What is it like for them, how painful is it? Think of concrete actions you could take to adjust your approach. Are there blocks inside yourself that you have to work on before moving to action? Do you wonder why they can't just get over it?

Take the first steps.

Conclusion

All our meditations have been about getting to the JUSTICE-LOVE that heals divisions between people and cultures. Have they helped? Are we on the way to being reconcilers?

We've removed some of the obstacles that have stood in our way and have found a more reliable direct route. We know now that mere sentimentality won't do the trick and we can't rely on good intentions and warm feelings. We know we should be more kind but we know that kindness alone is not enough.

But hopefully, we've glimpsed the possibility of a shocking, mind-blowing kind of healing love that grows from the hard work of honest self-reflection and personal accountability, and thrives on radical empathy towards and deep esteeming of others.

Why have we tried to "Be still and know..."? To temporarily block the noise around us so we can see our own blocks to loving and healing. To be honest about our common cultural arrogance, which so often stops us from learning about another person or group's pain. And in that stillness, to cultivate our truest, most grounded selves with the capacity for healing, reconciling, inviting, including and speaking truth to power.

We have meditated on our humanity because it is what we all share. And begun to grow in ourselves the radical empathy that esteems rather than demeans other human beings and values them in the full context of their history and experience.

We have thought of another's reality as the "holy of holies" and of each person as a sacred "Thou" rather than an "It."

We've learned too that it's OK to be frustrated about the many times our good intentions evaporate into thin air. Join the club!

But the work must go on. We must never abandon the wonderful stirrings within us to be part of the way of love and peace. We must continue to "be still" and discover (and rediscover) our blocks to healing love.

Then — and only then — will we know the "right" actions to take so that we are more likely than before to bring Justice-Love, the LOVE THAT HEALS, to fruition.

Perhaps the biggest question of all is: "Will we engage in the process of reconciliation or will we remain complicit in what brings division and conflict?"

Hopefully, our reflections have helped us notice how we may have unknowingly been complicit in personal or systemic injustice. We live in a web of relationships in which we are all responsible for each other at some level. Inevitably, our self-protectiveness, our defensiveness, crosses the line into unfairness.

As we have meditated and opened ourselves to our truth, perhaps we have been able to eliminate some of our own blocks to being generators of Justice-Love. Hopefully we have discovered new ways to overcome our own inner resistance to getting involved in the healing process. Maybe we have a better awareness of the importance of giving the gift of attention to those we aspire to love — the gifts of deep looking and deep listening. Perhaps new resolve, energy and competence have taken the place of what previously was merely good intention.

If so, that is cause for celebration and thanksgiving.

No one is asking us to grovel in the dirt and proclaim how terrible we are! Calm self-honesty is what this is all about. As Joan Baez has sung, "There but for fortune go you or I!" (Ochs, 1963) Compassion. Human connection. How can we move from "us versus them," "me versus you," to the reconciling love that heals?

Our communities are crying out for the healing of so many hurts, the reconciling of so many broken relationships, the restoring of a state of justice where little justice has prevailed. We all have the responsibility to position ourselves honestly and lovingly in this web of hurts crying out for healing.

Conclusion

What healing action can we take? Are we willing to ask ourselves the hard questions about our own complicity? Our own passivity? It's hard work to develop that kind of openness. That's what this book has tried to help with initiating. We will never be finished — Justice-Love is always a work-in-Progress!

The best endings invite new beginnings. Is there a new beginning here for you? Have your reflections given you a glimpse of what inner work you can do to equip yourself for, and propel yourself toward the kind of loving action that heals and reconciles?

Of course, you could simply close and shelve this short book and find it in a few months or years. "Oh!" you might say. "I meant to do something about that but I forgot all about it".

Don't we all do that rather too often?

And you could pick up the next highly recommended "must-read" book and "educate" yourself even more about what needs to be done. But you already know…

I invite you to do something different this time. Keep this book nearby for a while. Glance back over the chapter titles, the reflections, the notes you made. Where did you see your particular blocks, your growth in understanding? What struck you as having significant bearing on your development as a courageous practitioner of the Justice-Love that heals?

———

"Each day we practice looking deeply into ourselves and into the situation of our brothers and sisters. It is the most serious work we can do."
~ Thich Nhat Hanh ~

"We will rebuild, reconcile, and recover,
In every known nook of our nation,
In every corner called our country,
Our people, diverse and dutiful.
We'll emerge, battered but beautiful.
When day comes, we step out of the shade,
Aflame and unafraid.
The new dawn blooms as we free it,
For there is always light,
If only we're brave enough to see it,
If only we're brave enough to be it."

~ Amanda Gorman ~

Excerpted from
"The Hill We Climb:
An Inaugural Poem for the Country."
2021

Resources

We are trying in a practical down-to-earth way to learn to be more loving. Sometimes we read too many books about things we strongly aspire to, as if the depth of immersion by itself is going to change us. That can intellectualize, dilute and dissipate the transformative power of the self-reflection that is the true core of inner transformation.

Give priority to the self-reflection encouraged in each chapter of this book. For many of us, that next book or video can be an easy distraction or novelty that takes us away from the crucial inner work we really need to do, perhaps deep down actually want to do, but which keeps somehow getting away from us. Dedicated honest self-reflection is what we need to help us understand our own best next steps to being reconcilers!

Having said this, however, here are some resources that have been and continue to be helpful in my own journey toward Justice-Love.

Mindfulness and Self-Reflection: The first few chapters of this book invite you to "be still" and open and self-reflective. Perhaps you are already well-equipped for this because of prior experience with forms of mindfulness or meditation. If this is new to you, however, you may want to use some brief and simple text or audio to guide you.

Thich Nhat Hanh or Pema Chödrön's shorter texts or audios may be of considerable help. Hanh's book *Creating True Peace* (2004) is especially in line with the goals of this manual because his modeling of deep self-reflection is infectious, inspiring and practical. His book *Living Buddha, Living Christ* (1997) is helpful because it models the way we can courageously reflect on any smugness or arrogance about our own faiths or cultures while still treasuring them.

Ubuntu and Human Connection: Ubuntu is not a new concept —
but Desmond Tutu is largely responsible for bringing it
back into prominence. He lived it and taught it. I strongly
recommend his writings as a place to get a deeper sense of its
importance for "Justice-Love"!

I barely scratched the surface of Martin Buber's deep reflection on
relationships of utmost mutual respect. His classic *I and Thou* may
be worth a read, but for our purposes, it is the concept of deep,
mutual, non-judgmental respect and your willingness to meditate
on it that is most important. We already have more than enough
to convince us of our shared humanity. What we need is the quiet
and the focus to embrace it and live it.

Firming Up a True, Healthy, Differentiated Self: The brief
discussion of self-differentiation mentioned here is important in
our growth process but it is just the tip of the iceberg, enough to
help you self-reflect and open yourself to your unique growth
possibilities. In case a bit more clarification is needed to help
you in that process, I suggest "A Short Introduction to Bowen
Theory in His Own Words," The Murray Bowen Archives
Project, available at *murraybowenarchives.org*.

I have shared enough to open up for you an important area of
self-reflection. The critical thing is to enter that process with as
much honesty, enthusiasm and resolve as you can muster. That
could well lead you in the most important direction you need
to go right now without reading more books and learning more
theory.

Faith – Both Resource and Potential Obstacle: One's faith, spiritual background and moral underpinnings can be tremendous resources for, and motivators of, healing love. But it can also be an obstacle to the openness needed for the "esteeming" of another person or group. It's easy to claim that our culture, faith and/or life philosophy is the best one for generating love. What's more challenging is to have the courage and honesty to reflect on and critique the ways in which we may have blind spots about that.

Religion is a good example. By now it is well-documented and well-known how much arrogant and self-righteous religion has contributed to war and division instead of to the healing of division. Instead of more books and arguments about this, I suggest more courageous self-reflection and self-honesty about ways our faith or culture may aid and abet division instead of fostering mutual respect and healing.

Cultural Stuckness and Cultural Humility: The chapter on "Cultural Humility" may be the most important chapter in this book. Hopefully our reflections have made us more able to recognize stuckness and regression in our personal growth journeys. But what is not nearly as easy to recognize is what we have described as "cultural stuckness." For professional healers who want deeper insights about this, I recommend what I consider to be one of the best human development theory books ever written: Robert Kegan's *The Evolving Self* (1982).

But most of us don't have to get that technical to benefit from our reflections. To deepen our awareness and develop cultural humility in a wonderfully motivating way, I recommend Robin Kimmerer's *Braiding Sweetgrass* (2013).

Citations for Chapter Heading Quotations

1 – "Each day we practice looking deeply into ourselves and into the situation of our brothers and sisters. It is the most serious work we can do." Thich Nhat Hanh. *Living Buddha, Living Christ* (1997).

2 – "Compassion becomes real when we recognize our shared humanity." Pema Chödrön, *The Places that Scare You* (2018).

3 – "This is the Holy of Holies" Ezekiel 41:4, Jewish Publication Society TANAKH (The New JPS Translation according to the Traditional Hebrew Text, 1985.)

4 – "Take off your shoes: you are in the sacred valley…" Qur'an 20:12.

5 – "Be still and know…" Psalm 46 NRSV.

6 – "The more I wonder, the more I love." Alice Walker. *The Color Purple* (2018).

7 – "A genuine spiritual life is a continuous, daily struggle for freedom and liberation." Albert Nolan: *Biblical Spirituality* (1986).

8 – "Meaning arises not in either subject or object, but in the shared wisdom…that arises in the "between"… Pamela Cooper-White: *Shared Wisdom* (2004).

9 – "We all have an infant inside of us, but the infant doesn't have to run the show!" Murray Bowen. Widely and credibly quoted, exact citation unknown.

10 – "To be rooted is perhaps the most important and least recognized need of the human soul." Simone Weil, *The Need for Roots* (2002).

11 – "Attention is the rarest form of generosity." Simone Weil, as quoted by Vetö Miklos.

12 – "Diversity is being invited to the party; inclusion is being asked to dance." Verna Myers, "Diversity and Inclusion."

13 – "Love is not a weak, spineless emotion; it is a powerful moral force on the side of justice." Bernice A. King, CEO of The King Center. @BerniceKing twitter quote on 10/08/2020.

14 – "There is no way to peace. Peace *is* the way." A.J. Muste, as quoted in the title of Scott Ward's review of Danielson's *American Gandhi: A.J. Muste and the History of Radicalism* (2014).

Bibliography

Bowen, Murray. "A Short Introduction to Bowen Theory in His Own Words." *The Murray Bowen Archives Project.* murraybowenarchives. org.

Buber, Martin. 1970. *I and Thou.* Translation by Walter Kaufmann, Charles Scribner's Sons, New York, 1970.

Bethge, Eberhard and Renate Bethge. Quoted from personal notes and recollection of a "Christian Institute" meeting in Durban, South Africa, 1973.

Chödrön, Pema. 2018. *The Places That Scare You : A Guide to Fearlessness in Difficult Times.* Random House Inc.

Cooper-White, Pamela. 2004. *Shared Wisdom.* Fortress Press.

Danielson, Leilah. 2014. *American Gandhi : A.J. Muste and the History of Radicalism in the Twentieth Century.* Philadelphia: University Of Pennsylvania Press.

Frankl, Viktor. 2006. *Man's Search for Meaning.* Boston: Beacon Press.

Friedman, Edwin. 1985. *Generation to Generation, Family Process in Church and Synagogue.* New York: The Guilford Press.

Garofalo, Michael. gardendigest.com/awe.htm#Quotes. Numerous quotes on Awe and Wonder compiled by Michael Garofalo, Greenway Research, Valley Spirit Center, Red Bluff, California.

Gorman, Amanda. 2021. *The Hill We Climb and Other Poems.* S.L.: Viking Children's Books.

Hanh, Thich Nhat. 2004. *Creating True Peace, Ending Violence in Yourself, Your Family, Your Community, and the World*: New York: Free Press (Simon and Schuster).

Hanh, Thich Nhat. 1997. *Living Buddha, Living Christ.* New York: Riverhead Books.

Kegan, Robert. 1982. *The Evolving Self*, Cambridge, Mass.: Harvard University Press.

Kimmerer, Robin Wall. 2013. *Braiding Sweetgrass: Indigenous Wisdom, Scientific Knowledge and the Teachings of Plants.* S.L.: Penguin Books.

King, Bernice. "Love is not a weak, spineless emotion......." Quoted in *Sojourners Magazine* as the "Sojourners Voice of the Day" for 12/14/21.

Muste, A.J. 2014. "There is no way to peace…" Quoted in the title of Scott Ward's review of *American Gandhi: A.J. Muste and the History of Radicalism in the Twentieth Century.*

Myers, Verna. "Diversity and Inclusion," The Verna Myers Company Website: vernamyers.com. Myers famous quote: "Diversity is being invited to the party; inclusion is being asked to dance."

Mungi Ngomane. 2020. *Everyday Ubuntu : Living Better Together, the African Way.* New York, NY: Harper Design.

Nolan, Albert. 1986. *Biblical Spirituality, Lecture Notes for Annual Faith and Life Course*, Order of Preachers, Springs, South Africa.

Ochs, Phil. 1963. "There but for Fortune." Covered by Joan Baez.

O'Donohue, John. 1999. *Anam Cara: Spiritual Wisdom from the Celtic World.* Bantam Books.

Oxhandler, Holly. 2022. *The Soul of the Helper.* Templeton Foundation Press.

Tervalon, Melanie and Murray-Garcia, Jann. "Cultural Humility versus Cultural Competence: A Critical Distinction in Defining Physician Training Outcomes in Multicultural Education," *Journal of Health Care for the Poor and Underserved*, Volume 9, Number 2, May 1998, pp 117-125.

Sparks, Allister, and Mpho Tutu. 2011. *Tutu: Authorized.* Harper Collins.

Suzman, Helen. 1993. *In No Uncertain Terms.* NY: Knopf.

Tutu, Desmond. *The Rainbow People of God, the making of a peaceful revolution*, NY, Doubleday, 1994.

Vetö, Miklos. *The Religious Metaphysics of Simone Weil* (translated by Joan Dargan), State University of NY Press, Albany 1994.

Walker, Alice. 2018. *The Color Purple*, London, Orion Publishing.

Wilkerson, Isabel. 2020. Caste. [S.I.]: Random House Publishing Group.

Winnicott, D.W. 2012. *Playing and Reality.* Routledge.

Weil, Simone: 2002. *The Need for Roots.* Translated by Arthur Wills, Routledge Classics, London and New York 2002. Famous Weil quote on page 40: "To be rooted is perhaps the most important and least recognized need of the human soul."

Appreciations

This project is dedicated with love and gratitude....

To Jane, the best loving partner anyone could have. You've taught me so much about being truly present, about healing, and about love. And you've loved me that way!

To my beloved children Anthony, Libby, Megan and James who put up with the fact that my loving and fathering were (and are still) a work in progress.

To my fellow clinicians, healers and clergy colleagues of different faiths and persuasions. You exemplified competence and service without forfeiting love.

To the many therapy clients, parishioners and supervisees that it was my privilege to serve. You trusted me, you taught me about love, you helped me keep growing.

To Dean Rene John and my fellow members of Trinity Cathedral in Trenton. Joyfully we have broken bread together. You've taught me authentic community with its joys and sorrows, mutual accountability and abiding love.

To my late parents Mom and Dad, and my late siblings Anthony, Michael and Margaret, and Kathleen who keeps on going, and my nephew and many nieces—your faith and service have inspired me, and your love has upheld me.

Acknowledgments

This manuscript may well have stayed on the shelf were it not for the encouragement of Tom Tisdale and the tireless shaping of Vally Sharpe. Thank you.

And, thank you to Noor Phillips, Clara Gregory, Lisa Schwartz, Georgia Koenig, Elyse Smith, Kimme Carlos, Melanie Nolan, Dan Whitener, La'Tonya Johnson, John O'Hagan, Sister Brigid Rose Tiernan, Sister Marie André Mitchell, Marist Brothers, Notre Dame de Namur Sisters, and the Trinity Cathedral African Festival Committee: You have all helped and inspired me in significant ways.

About the Author

Born in South Africa and ordained a priest in 1965, PETER BRIDGE's early ministry included serving rural mission outstations, urban communities, teaching and activism. Earning his Bachelor's Degree in Social Science (Unisa University) involved a Social Work internship in the now famous Black township of Soweto. He describes that experience together with an exposé he wrote about one of the government's nefarious resettlement schemes which reached parliament, as turning points in his life. He became a member of the Christian Institute whose members—from all faiths and races— opposed the apartheid government, and predictably, became the target of various forms of government suppression.

Peter was awarded an International Institute of Education Scholarship and graduated with a Masters in Social Work (MSW) at Rutgers University and a Doctor of Ministry (D.Min) at Lancaster Theological Seminary. In the US, he continued his ministry of healing and reconciliation in individual, couple and group settings, as a Licensed Clinical Social Worker and Certified Pastoral Psychotherapist. Besides congregational and non-profit consulting and clergy coaching, he was mentor and supervisor to numerous therapists. He held teaching positions at the Pastoral Training Institute and Moravian Theological Seminary where he developed the Masters in Pastoral Counseling Program. Well known for his work in Relationship and Family Therapy and Supervision, he has presented at the national conventions of both the American Psychological Association and the American Association for Marriage and Family Therapy. He is a former chairperson of the Bucks County (PA) Mental Health Board on which he served for 17 years.

During his tenure as President of the Pennsylvania Association for Marriage and Family Therapy, major strides were made in the effort, soon successful, to enact licensure for Professional Counselors and Marriage and Family Therapists. He was awarded the Samaritan Spirit Award for outstanding service to the community.

For the past 22 years, Peter has served as a volunteer Associate Priest at Trinity Episcopal Cathedral in Trenton, New Jersey. He describes that community as a cherished and fulfilling part of his life. He credits his wife Jane, their four children, and eight grandchildren as the "real seminary" of his life. "They have taught me about love and life's true priorities," he says.

Peter and Jane have two life mottoes: "Namaste!" (I greet the divine in you!), and the psalm verse: "Today is the day the Lord has made. Exult and Rejoice in it!"

GUIDE FOR STUDY/DISCUSSION GROUP

Four Sessions
90 minutes each

Interfaith/Intercultural Groups are
Strongly Encouraged

Guide for Group Leaders/Facilitators:

It is suggested that each session begin with an invitation to "Be Still and Know..." — an invitation to a silent gathering of thoughts, grounding in the present moment, leaving behind the distractions of the day (not more than 5 minutes).

At the beginning of each session, facilitator remarks should be **very brief** so as not to limit time for group participation.

Encourage participants to engage in "small group" activities with different people each session.

Suggest participants keep their "main takeaway" and "action" notes in their copies of the Justice-Love book for further reflection and implementation.

At the end of each session, remind participants about the next session's readings.

Session One

Preparatory Reading (prior to the session): Read the "Introduction" with special focus on the explanations of "Self-Reflection" and "Other-Reflection." Also read Chapter 5: "Be Still and Know..."

15 minutes: Facilitator gives a brief overview/reminder of what the author discussed in the Introduction about Self-Reflection and Other-Reflection, and how "Be Still and Know...." factors into Reflection.

30 minutes: Small groups form and share their reactions, especially to what they find helpful and/or challenging about the two kinds of reflection.

30 minutes: Report back to the full group and continue discussion in plenary.

15 minutes: Participants are invited to ponder silently and write down, for their own use, their main takeaway from the session and actions they may take.

_____

_____

_____

_____

_____

_____

_____

_____

Session Two

Preparatory Reading (prior to the session): Chapters 2, 3, 4 and 6, focusing on the ways in which "shared humanity," "entering the 'holy of holies' of another person's world," "removing one's shoes in a person/group's sacred space," and "awe and gratitude" bring people together.

15 minutes: Facilitator gives a brief overview/reminder of the way the above concepts can move people toward Justice-Love.

30 minutes: Small groups form and share their reactions to the above concepts.

30 minutes: Report back to the full group and continue discussion in plenary.

15 minutes: Participants are invited to ponder silently and write down, for their own use, their main takeaway from the session and actions they may take.

_____

_____

_____

_____

_____

_____

_____

_____

Session Three

Preparatory Reading (prior to the session): Read Chapters 7 through 10 focusing on the ways cultural "stuckness," a lack of shared meaning, difficulty growing one's own authentic self, and being ungrounded can inhibit one's growth toward Justice-Love.

> **15 minutes:** Facilitator gives a brief overview/reminder of the way the above issues can inhibit one's growth toward Justice-Love.

> **30 minutes:** Small groups form and share their reactions to the above concepts.

> **30 minutes:** Report back to the full group and continue discussion in plenary.

> **15 minutes:** Participants are invited to ponder silently and write down, for their own use, their main takeaway from the session and actions they may take.

Session Four

Preparatory Reading (prior to the session): Read the remaining chapters, focusing especially on your own feelings as you become increasingly aware of the many blocks to justice and reconciliation in ourselves, our culture and our society. Then write down any new thoughts about actions you might take.

15 minutes: Facilitator gives a brief overview/reminder of the many cultural and societal blocks to the development of Justice-Love in these chapters.

30 minutes: Small groups form and share their reactions to the "blocks" to Justice-Love touched on in these chapters.

30 minutes: Report back to the full group and continue discussion in plenary.

15 minutes: Participants are invited to ponder silently and write down, for their own use, their main takeaway from the session and actions they may take.

_____

_____

_____

_____

_____

_____

_____

_____

_____

Additional Notes

Made in the USA
Middletown, DE
26 March 2024

51916039R00070